rebuilding communities in a refugee settlement

A Casebook from Uganda

Lina Payne

Oxfam GB

facing page April 1996: registration of new arrivals in Imvepi

© Oxfam GB 1998
First published by Oxfam GB 1998

A catalogue record for this publication is available from the British Library.

ISBN 0 855983 94 9

Available from the following agents:
for Canada and the USA: Humanities Press International, 165 First Avenue, Atlantic Highlands, New Jersey NJ 07716-1289, USA; tel. 732 872 1441; fax. 732 872 0717
for Southern Africa: David Philip Publishers, PO Box 23408, Claremont, Cape Town 7735, South Africa; tel. (021) 644136; fax. (021) 643358
for Australia: Bush Books, PO Box 1370, Gosford South, NSW 2250, Australia; tel. (043) 233274; fax. (029) 212248
for the rest of the world, contact: Oxfam Publishing, 274 Banbury Road, Oxford OX2 7DZ, UK

Published by Oxfam GB, 274 Banbury Road, Oxford OX2 7DZ

JB005/RB/98
Printed by Oxfam Print Unit

Oxfam GB is registered as a charity, no. 202918, and is a member of Oxfam International.

Front cover photo: Jenny Matthews/Oxfam

Oxfam/Jenny Matthews

Contents

This book is dedicated to the memory of the nine staff of Oxfam Ikafe and Imvepi
who died as a result of illness during the course of the programme.
And to Juma Musa, who died while serving displaced refugees in Yumbe.

Acknowledgements

It is impossible to acknowledge everyone who contributed to this book. Most of the analysis is the outcome of long discussions with many Sudanese refugees in Ikafe and Imvepi, and so my thanks are due firstly to all those who were so open and trusting in sharing their ideas and experiences. I hope they will feel that I have been faithful to them. Thanks are due also to the 15 Sudanese members of the Research Team in Ikafe, and to the many Oxfam staff in Imvepi who gave up time to discuss various aspects of the book. The fact that Imvepi is such a strong programme today is a credit to the Sudanese refugees who never gave up, and who taught Oxfam staff to take every situation as it comes. And it is thanks also to a few members of staff who struggled through very hard times to set the programme back on its feet.

A few individuals must be mentioned by name. Grace Mbabazi, with whom I shared a *tukul* in Imvepi, did much to keep my spirits up through often difficult times. Faisa Ring contributed valuable insights from the Sudanese perspective. Izzy Birch gave unceasing support to the Ikafe/Imvepi programme as a whole; and to me while I was writing this book. Thanks are due also to Judy Adoko for her encouragement; to Tony Burdon for reading and commenting on a number of drafts; to Jamie Balfour-Paul for his very useful input, and also to Simon Ameny. In Oxfam House, Maurice Herson, Nick Leader, Koos Neefjes, Caroline Sweetman, and Helen Young found time to read through early drafts, and each made extremely helpful observations. I hope that all these busy people will feel that I have managed to justify the time they spent on the project.

Thanks are due also to Godwin Soro for producing the maps in this book, to Muhammed in MSF, Leonard Okello and Patrick Bamuzi (among others) for trying to make sure there was power in Imvepi when supplies were short, and to Joseph for all his help with copying and computers.

To everyone who contributed but is not mentioned here, my apologies — and again my thanks.

Lina Payne
Oxford, May 1998

Abbreviations

AAIN	Action Africa in Need (a German NGO)
CBO	Community-Based Organisation
CBR	Community-Based Rehabilitation
GoS	Government of Sudan
GoU	Government of Uganda
JRS	Jesuit Refugee Service
LC	Local Council
MoLG	Ministry of Local Government
MoU	Memorandum of Understanding
NGOs	Non-government Organisations
Oxfam House	Oxfam's head office (Oxford)
RSP	Refugee Studies Programme, Oxford University
SPLA	Sudan People's Liberation Army
SPLM	Sudan People's Liberation Movement
WNBF	West Nile Bank Front

Preface

Agencies working with displaced people are often keen to explore sustainable responses to the growing 'refugee problem': more durable forms of support than those offered by the traditional camp, with its focus on care and maintenance. The impetus comes from donors wanting to encourage self-sufficiency as a cheaper alternative to high-input relief programmes; and from non-government organisations (NGOs) interested in strengthening fragmented communities from the grassroots up.

The Ikafe/Imvepi settlement in a remote corner of northern Uganda is a case in point. On this site, Oxfam GB has worked with refugees from south Sudan since 1994 to establish an integrated development programme. Around 55,000 people were settled in Ikafe/Imvepi and given the opportunity to cultivate food for themselves and to develop livelihoods — all in an area of bush with virtually no infrastructure. The programme aimed in the short term to provide 'effective management of services, rooted in gender-aware analysis' and to facilitate refugee participation in camp activities; while in the longer term it aimed to promote self-reliance for refugees and to integrate the project into local Ugandan structures.

In Ikafe/Imvepi, Oxfam tried to go further than simply sustaining a population in passive dependence on international aid. Instead of the all-too-common relationship between powerful donor and dependent recipients, Oxfam wanted to see refugees taking some control of their own lives. The agency had a vision of a self-reliant population, co-existing with local people in small and well-spaced communities: a refugee population who might eventually live independently of any external assistance.

To achieve this goal would involve challenging conventional ways of giving relief assistance, developing ways of working so that capacity for self-managed, sustainable livelihoods would be built up at the community level right from the outset. It meant trying to foster participation and capacity-building — the type of work more often associated with projects labelled as 'development' work — while meeting the demands of donors for high-input, tangible results on the ground. Adopting 'a more developmental approach to emergency work' was a key objective for Ikafe/Imvepi.

The Ikafe/Imvepi programme very clearly illustrates how hard it is to implement activities which address simultaneously the immediate needs and the longer-term requirements of displaced communities. It exposed all the strains of trying to implement plans that attract different kinds of funding and require a range of staff with distinct skills and ways of working. The 'Ikafe experience' has led Oxfam staff to question the utility of categorising programmes within the specific framework of 'relief' or 'development'. In Ikafe, it was simply not possible to confine activities within such tight definitions. 'Relief' and 'development' might appear to be fundamentally different — one being concerned to preserve life or livelihoods, and the other intended to induce change — but the differences are essentially theoretical: particularly in the turbulent climate of the 1990s, there is much more room for convergence between the two than for division.

The main need of vulnerable communities, whatever their situation, is to develop their capacity to cope with uncertainty. Good systems of communication are essential, to facilitate dialogue between the refugees, the host population, donors, and governments. Supporting agencies need good staff who are prepared to adapt, and flexible systems which are able to accommodate change.

If the experience of the Ikafe/Imvepi programme has shown anything, it has underlined the importance of being *realistic* about what can be achieved. In Ikafe/Imvepi, the working environment was never stable. There was always the challenge of creating the foundation for long-term structural change within an extremely short time-frame and in a very insecure situation; conditions were never 'normal'. There were constant differences of opinion among donors and partners about the definition of objectives and appropriate ways of working. Staff were always battling against pressures of time which left no space to think creatively. It was difficult to recruit the right sort of people to some sectors, and later on there were extreme financial constraints — all this in a context of extreme insecurity. At the same time, refugees were constantly weighing up whether or not to leave Ikafe, which sometimes frustrated their commitment to participating in the programme, and so compromised Oxfam's ability to function effectively.

A significant degree of NGO programming these days is implemented in situations that can best be described as turbulent, whether because of protracted conflict, environmental change, or general shifts in the economic and social climate. Even 'development' programmes in apparently conflict-free regions often find themselves struggling through periods of extreme uncertainty — especially in the ever-changing climate of structural adjustment programmes, or increasingly as the less tangible effects of the HIV/AIDS epidemic take hold. All too often there is no time to plan ways of involving vulnerable communities in capacity-building programmes, whether the context is conventionally described as 'relief' or a 'development'.

This book makes suggestions which are directly relevant to the management of refugee programmes: for example, how to involve communities in the development of life-saving systems such as water and food distribution right from the outset, in a way which will allow activities to continue even when an agency is forced to withdraw. The book also raises a series of questions. Is it possible, for example, to create the space to be radical, to shift from handouts to targeting, or to put proper representation into practice, in a turbulent situation such as Ikafe/Imvepi, where staff on the ground were almost always reacting to new circumstances, and there was hardly ever the opportunity to develop a more considered approach? The book also considers a number of broader issues related to the external environment in which Ikafe was operating: the policies and practices of donors and governments; the priorities of the refugees; and the concerns of the host population. It examines ways of reconciling some of these conflicts in the real world. In the words of Oxfam's former Country Representative in Uganda: '*An enabling environment for settlement is the "perfect world" picture. What can be done better in the existing environment?*'

There are no easy answers. This book may help agencies in similar circumstances to predict potential pressures and gear up more effectively to cope with the practical dilemmas they are likely to face — problems of administrative structures, staff recruitment and training, funding and accounting, and logistical problems. It also offers some guidance on ways of responding to a wider range of challenges, in terms of ensuring participation, representation, and gender equity, through a more considered approach to policy and programming work.

A note on the text

This casebook reflects the views of very many people, especially refugees and Oxfam staff from all sorts of backgrounds, who have contributed their ideas very freely through informal discussion. Throughout the text, however, none of the refugees or Oxfam staff is named in full. The situation remains highly political, and refugees returning to Sudan have sometimes been made to answer for their actions and words during the time they were settled in Uganda. Similarly, many local staff were reluctant to have their ideas put in print while still employed by Oxfam on the Imvepi programme. Where appropriate, individual members of staff are identified by the titles of the posts which they held at the time when they were interviewed for this book.

Although the casebook builds on the ideas of many different people, inevitably it is presented from the perspective of the writer. Many of the issues discussed are extremely complex and highly sensitive. UNHCR, the Government of Uganda, other agencies involved, and not least other Oxfam staff would no doubt have different views on many of the issues. They are all equally valid. None of the opinions expressed in the text is intended to give offence. They are offered with the aim of sharing experience and lessons learned.

On reading the first draft of this text, a number of people commented on its negative tone. Perhaps I should state explicitly from the outset that the Ikafe/Imvepi programme was notable for some extremely positive achievements in a very short and extremely difficult period. Oxfam staff addressed the needs of thousands of refugees at very short notice in what turned out to be an extremely demanding emergency, both in the early days of settlement, and later on during the year of insecurity. There was never any serious outbreak of disease at any time — something that was always a risk in the heavily overcrowded transit areas. By the end of 1995, thousands of refugees had built their own homes, and had begun to contribute to their own livelihoods. Before the onset of insecurity, the Ikafe/Imvepi settlement offered a real breathing space, and the chance for many families to consider a more settled future.

During that process many lessons were learned by those Oxfam staff and their managers who were willing to listen to the refugees and representatives of the host population. It is a credit to their commitment and professionalism that they were willing and able to make changes to the programme as the situation evolved. One member of staff remarked: '*Through learning, we realise how far we have come, but equally how far we have to go.*'

Since the experiences and lessons outlined in the text are relevant to both settlements, throughout this book 'Ikafe' will be used to refer to both the Ikafe and Imvepi programmes, except where issues are relevant directly and solely to the Imvepi programme.

Introduction

Why settlement programmes?

Settlement programmes, in contrast to refugee transit camps, seek to provide an opportunity for refugees to become more independent, by giving them a chance to develop their own livelihoods, and integrating them within the official structures and systems of the host population. They were first promoted in the early 1960s, and between then and the late 1980s over 100 were established around the world, with varying degrees of success. Since 1987, however, there has been a shift in UNHCR policy to promote voluntary repatriation as a first preference in refugee situations, and a reluctance to make commitments to programmes like 'Ikafe'. It was the protracted nature of the conflict in Sudan which led UNHCR, with the Government of Uganda (GoU), to look for a more durable solution to the Sudanese refugee problem. The task was made easier by the fact that the Ugandan Government has always had extremely generous policies on the acceptance of refugees, which allowed the option of a planned land-based rural settlement to be considered.

What is particularly attractive to donors about settlement programmes like Ikafe is the fact that they offer a cheaper longer-term option in comparison with the more familiar care-and-maintenance 'transit' camps. African governments and international donors are tired of supporting endless transits, where money seems to be poured down a bottomless pit. They need to achieve major savings in the provision of food and other aid, especially in the chronic emergencies where there is no obvious end in sight — the civil war in South Sudan being a prime example. At the time when the Ikafe programme was established, pressures were even greater, because of the growing numbers of refugees around the world and especially in the Great Lakes region.

For a host government, settlement programmes represent an opportunity to obtain substantial infrastructural support, through the construction of schools, health centres, boreholes, and roads, which all serve to improve the general economy of an area. They also offer a chance to avoid some of the environmental problems created by many transit situations, through the adoption of a more ordered settlement process and a more holistic approach, whereby sectoral activities like agriculture or sanitation are approached from a long-term perspective that focuses on sustainable solutions.

For agencies like Oxfam GB (hereafter referred to as 'Oxfam'), a settlement programme also provides the opportunity to enhance the dignity of vulnerable populations, by encouraging their participation in rehabilitation programmes — something which is not possible in transit camps, which offer little scope for self-reliance or even self-management of community affairs.

The longer-term approach in a programme like Ikafe offers a chance to tackle some of these challenges. Providing the opportunity for refugees to settle as family units which can identify themselves with the community around them, and giving households a means to provide for their own livelihoods can help them to re-establish their self-respect. Such opportunities are often not present in the more common care-and-maintenance camps.

Oxfam's perspective

In Oxfam's experience, people are often poorly served in refugee situations, for a variety of reasons. Poor overall management, government inaction on legal matters such as land allocation, divisions between NGOs, inadequate refugee representation, and a short-term approach to long-term problems have all worked in various ways to create obstacles to building up refugees' own capabilities.

In the Ikafe programme, it was hoped to minimise these problems by using Oxfam's approach to development as a starting point. This would mean bringing a thorough gender analysis into all aspects of work, involving communities in planning and making decisions, and putting emphasis on refugee representation. It would imply a more considered approach to developing livelihoods, one that promoted self-reliance in a sustainable way, by avoiding damage to the natural environment and taking account of the needs of the host population.

Interviewed for this book, Oxfam's Country Representative in Uganda during the establishment of the Ikafe programme explained his prime concerns:

> ❡ I wanted us to do wider emergency work — not just water, but integrated ways of working. Much of this ranged around a desire to deal with food distribution as a way to 'empower' refugees through self-management of these systems. I wanted us to work hard at promoting refugee representation, since this has generally been done poorly, in my experience. By establishing an integrated programme, we would be able

to cover a wide range of areas and promote representation in all. I also wanted us to address gender properly throughout, rather than pay lip-service to it. There was also an interest to learn from our development work in Uganda and elsewhere, such that we could try to address the move from relief to development, and look at interesting ways to do that. We also hoped for some form of development inputs for the host community, in addition to the more refugee-focused infrastructure. We used it as an opportunity for staff development too ... and for organisational learning. **⁊**

Oxfam had good resources in Uganda, particularly in terms of staff and skills, so it was in a favourable position to respond quickly, especially with technical inputs. Work was already going on to provide water and sanitation in Koboko, a refugee camp in Arua District close to the border with South Sudan, from where refugees were due to be transferred by UNHCR and GoU to the area of Ikafe. Staff already had experience of working with people from Southern Sudan in some of the transit camps in Kiriandongo settlement in the north of Uganda, where Oxfam provided emergency relief and general settlement support. In Kitgum and Karamoja, in the north and north-east, they had explored more participative ways of distributing food, seeds, and tools. They had also implemented a successful programme for non-food items across the whole District of Kitgum in the late 1980s.

For Oxfam, the adoption of a leading implementational role in a long-term programme of this nature reflected an organisational shift towards becoming more operational in multi-sectoral integrated programmes. While Oxfam has often implemented relief activities in emergencies, it has tended to specialise in particular sectors, especially water supplies and food distribution. The scope to explore more radical ways of developing the capacity of beneficiaries, for instance through proper representation or self-management in communal activities, has often been limited by the short-term nature of operations. Although in some cases Oxfam's long-term presence in a country has provided the opportunity to maintain some sort of operation after other agencies have pulled out, the fact that this has not been planned at the outset has meant that activities have tended to be more reactive — responding to a certain situation on the ground — and it has not always been possible to prioritise capacity-building for long-term self-reliance.

Oxfam has not often been fully operational in so-called 'development' or 'capacity-building' projects, choosing instead to give funding and technical support through established NGOs and community-based organisations (CBOs) as a more sustainable option. The presence of staff on the ground,

3

however, has allowed Oxfam to play a semi-operational role, and it is this role that is now expanding. In a number of countries, including Uganda, Oxfam is now much more involved in implementing longer-term integrated programmes to build community capacity.

Oxfam's relationship with funders has also begun to shift. The sheer scale of interventions between 1994 and 1997, in the Great Lakes and elsewhere, has obliged Oxfam to accept funding from major donors such as UNHCR and the European Union for emergency interventions. While this was not entirely new to Oxfam — major-donor funding for large-scale emergencies was accepted throughout the 1980s — it has been coupled with a growing fatigue among other donors, which has restricted Oxfam's own abilities to respond to crises using its own resources. Embarking on a programme of this size in partnership with UNHCR was not such a big issue. However, the unusual nature of the funding partnership (whereby Oxfam was at times receiving over 50 per cent of funding from a single donor) did threaten to compromise the agency's independence.

This casebook

Ikafe generated a huge amount of interest and excitement within Oxfam, especially in the early days. In the words of the Programme Support Manager for East Africa:

> ❦ [One cannot forget] the sheer excitement and novelty of the programme in 1994/5, and the energy that went into the establishment of the settlement. No one who visited Bidibidi in the first year of the programme could fail to come away without some feeling of this, and without some strong identification with what the team was trying (under very difficult circumstances) to achieve ... For me, it was one of the most exciting pieces of Oxfam work that I have witnessed. ❧

But it was also enormously time-consuming for staff from a number of different departments, including the many fund-raisers and emergency support staff at the head office (Oxfam House in Oxford, England).

Staff who were managing or advising on the programme were well aware of the common obstacles to successful settlement: problems such as hostile relations with the local population, or a climate of apathy among dependent refugees; they were also able to draw on a wealth of academic and practical experience. Yet Ikafe still ran into difficulties. This casebook looks at some of the lessons learned from the whole experience by staff employed in Ikafe in many different capacities. It identifies some of the problems encountered in developing and implementing a programme of this nature. The lessons are presented in a practical way, which it is hoped will contribute to the development of programme and management practice, and increase understanding of key policy issues for developing other settlement programmes.

The book is divided into eight chapters. The first gives a very broad overview of the programme, from inception through to the situation current in March 1998, to help readers to appreciate some of the problems as they are examined in later sections. Chapter 2 identifies a number of external factors which were always bound to affect the success of the programme, such as relationships between the host and refugee communities, and political, economic, and environmental matters.

Central to the vision of a sustainable settlement were the concepts of self-managed communities and self-reliant livelihoods that could function independently of any external assistance within a given time-frame. The remainder of the book considers how the programme in Ikafe tried to move towards this, in the context of (and sometimes despite) the overriding external factors.

Chapter 3 analyses Ikafe's approach to social reconstruction and self-management at the community level. The challenge in any programme of this nature is to develop the community's ability to function independently of agency support. Such work requires a particular approach, which is in many ways antithetical to the delivery of humanitarian relief services. Finding the space to involve communities, in a highly pressured environment, where basic needs must be addressed very quickly, is always difficult. The situation is not helped when people are highly disoriented, and may have lost their informal structures for organising themselves at the community level.

Chapter 4 then considers the development of sustainable livelihoods. The concept of self-reliance implies a much broader approach to the whole household economy than simply focusing on agriculture. Off-farm income opportunities were equally important in Ikafe, and became more so as communities were displaced from their original settlements. The programme also needed to ensure the self-reliance of the local population, because a refugee settlement never functions in an economic and physical vacuum. A strategy for developing livelihoods had to take into account the development of the natural resources, markets, and economy of the entire population — host and refugee.

An integrated approach is central, both to sustainable livelihoods and to self-managed communities. Refugee structures needed to be integrated within the Ugandan government's political, legal, and administrative systems, and within the more informal cultural systems at the local level, if they were to endure. To be sustainable, programme activities also needed to be linked to the strategies and operations of the relevant host-government departments. There is a note on this at the end of the fourth chapter.

Having looked at some of the programme inputs that can have an impact on the sustainability of the settlement, Chapter 5 then considers some of the other external factors which can compromise the objectives of a settlement programme. It considers in particular how some of the policies and practices of donors and governments may work to undermine self-management and weaken sustainable livelihoods.

The sixth chapter is concerned with particular approaches that can mitigate some of the more negative factors contributing to a 'disabling' environment. It focuses on issues of communication. Good communication was always key to the success of the programme in Ikafe, but was consistently compromised, mostly by the constant pressures of time. With so many 'stakeholders' involved, it was essential to reach agreement about responsibilities, objectives, and ways of working. Good communication also played an important part in helping refugees to take some control over their lives, ensuring that they had access to information which would enable them to make strategic choices which could affect their future capabilities. It was also key to the success of lobbying work.

Chapter 7 is concerned with organisational support. Agencies taking on similar programmes need to ask themselves whether they have the capacity, or are in a position to gear up to take on a project of this complexity. In Ikafe, for example, donors' funding and financial systems did not always give managers the flexibility to change planned activities, or the authority to take decisions. Planning needs to be supported by realistic objectives, and systems that will sound alarm bells and then facilitate change when the situation begins to alter. Particularly in turbulent situations, where the dynamics are never static, flexibility becomes crucial, and planning documents need to reflect this by making allowances for an ever-changing situation. But however good the systems, a programme ultimately relies on having high-calibre staff, who have the necessary 'people skills' and the vision and capacity to remain flexible. Yet there are inevitable difficulties in recruiting and retaining the right kind of staff, and ensuring a good gender balance, in such situations. National and refugee staff need personnel support that is specifically relevant to work in unusual situations like Ikafe.

The final chapter draws together some of the key lessons learned, and makes a few broad recommendations for future programmes.

An overview of the Ikafe programme I

Life before Ikafe

Sudanese people began to cross the border into Arua District of northern Uganda in August 1993. The movement marked an escalation of activities in the protracted war between the Government of Sudan (GoS) and various factions of the rebel Sudan People's Liberation Army (SPLA). Key areas close to the border which had previously been held by rebels had fallen to government forces, and huge numbers of people who had already been displaced from other parts of Yei District were forced to seek refuge in neighbouring Uganda. The Government of Uganda (GoU) believed that the situation would normalise relatively quickly, and the refugees were placed in temporary 'transit' (care and maintenance) camps in the border town of Koboko, where they began to establish lives based mostly on petty trading and piece-rate agricultural work. Oxfam was responsible for providing water and sanitation.

The refugee population in the Koboko camps continued to rise and had exceeded 100,000 by early 1994. There was no indication of a cessation of hostilities in Sudan; the natural environment around the transits was increasingly devastated; and the demand for humanitarian aid was enormous. The GoU began to look for other options to settle refugees.

There were also political reasons for wanting to move refugees farther from the border areas, which added to the sense of urgency. The presence of the Koboko camps just 14 kilometres from Sudan was seen as a real security risk; indeed, in 1996 Koboko was bombed by GoS forces. In 1993, the two governments accused each other of allowing weapons to be supplied through their respective countries to Ugandan and Sudanese rebel groups. The situation was politically tense, and the GoU wanted the camps broken up, to allay suspicions of rebel SPLA presence in Koboko. With an increasing number of incidents in early 1994 which were apparently aimed at discrediting the Ugandan authorities (including the killing in Arua town itself of some Europeans travelling in the region), and a series of abductions of refugees from the Koboko camps by warring rebel factions or by GoS forces, the Ugandan government resolved to move refugees immediately in order to improve security. It was hoped that settling refugees farther from the borders would reduce cross-border movement.

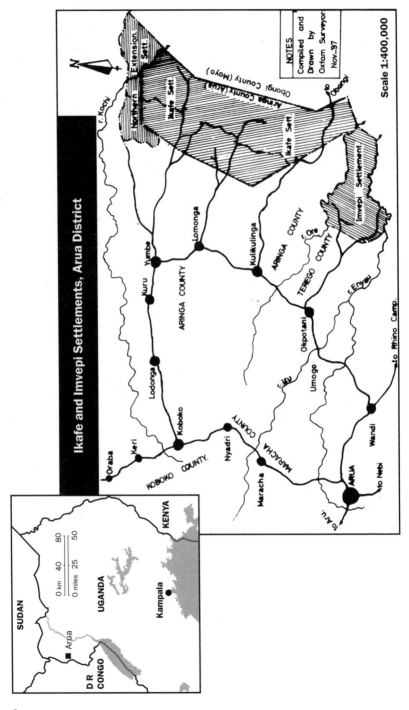

Ikafe and Imvepi Settlements, Arua District

Scale 1:400,000

NOTES
Compiled and Drawn by Oxfam Surveyor Nov—97

Government representatives negotiated with elders for land in the county of Aringa. Agreement was reached, but not on all aspects. Issues of compensation and land ownership were never clearly understood by the local landlords. At the time, the Aringas said that they were offering land to 'pay back their brothers' for the years in the 1980s when they themselves had been refugees and were hosted by some of the very same people who now found themselves in Uganda. There were also high (though initially unvoiced) expectations of development assistance, especially infrastructural support, and hopes of gaining from employment opportunities.

Discussions about the transfer of refugees to the area demarcated as 'Ikafe' were held in May 1994 between UNHCR and GoU officers in Kampala. No lead agency had been formally established at the time. Oxfam was not approached until August 1994, by which time pressure on UNHCR had increased dramatically, first to shift refugees from Koboko, and second to accommodate the hundreds of new refugees who had begun to arrive as new areas in Sudan were affected by the war.

Into the bush

Sited on the edge of the great East African Rift Valley, the stretch of land now known as Ikafe (named after a local tree) reaches about 37 km from north to south, and about 15 km across (east to west). It is a fairly barren land, with an unpredictable climate and rocky soils, except in areas close to the river beds and swamps where it drops down to the valley. Imvepi, which adjoins Ikafe on its extreme south-west border, is similar, though much smaller — just 15 km across in any direction — and a little more fertile, with the Enyau River flowing along its southern border before meeting the Nile. Both places have always been essentially uninhabited bush, used by local chiefs for hunting deer. Older people in the area can still recall tales of elephant hunts and rhino camps in the land now gazetted as Ikafe.

The northern and central parts of Ikafe, and much of Imvepi, were infested with tsetse fly before the refugees moved in; scorpions and poisonous snakes are still common throughout. Poor soils, lack of water, few roads, and the remote location have prevented all but a very small Ugandan population from inhabiting the area. In fact, within one season, there is often little trace of where a family may temporarily have settled or cultivated; the land quickly returns to bush, almost as if people were never really welcome there.

Ikafe falls within Aringa County, while Imvepi lies in the neighbouring county of Terego, both extremely underdeveloped areas within the economically deprived District of Arua. The entire District suffered widespread

9

destruction during the 1979/80 war which resulted in the overthrow of Idi Amin. The District had benefited considerably from his years in power; but, suddenly finding themselves the target of revenge from people and tribes in other parts of the country who had suffered under Amin, large numbers of Aringa sought refuge for most of the early 1980s in neighbouring Zaire or in Sudan. A visitor to Aringa county in 1982, for example, found just 300 inhabitants. Since that time, the area has never really recovered economically. The arrival of refugees was generally recognised as a good opportunity to attract development inputs.

Who are 'the refugees'?

The refugee population of Ikafe and Imvepi settlements was very mixed. In March 1995, there were almost equal numbers of women and men, 21,036 and 25,231 respectively, over 50 per cent of whom — some 23,510 — were under 16 years old. Around 40 per cent of households were registered as female-headed, but this may not be a very significant statistic, because many families were polygamous, and women registered alone often had husbands present somewhere else in the settlement. Men tended to be more mobile and maintained closer links across the border; as such, they often found it prudent to register their wives, who would be more likely to be present full-time to collect any entitlements. In addition, Oxfam made every effort to register wives in polygamous marriages individually, so that they would not miss any entitlements.

The refugees were ethnically mixed, with one tribe — the Kakwa — in the majority, though many of the other tribes from Yei District were also represented. Between 10 and 12 per cent were Dinka, a pastoral group mostly from the Bahr el Ghazal area north of Yei, who had few cultural or linguistic links with the majority Bari speakers. Most of the refugee population was Christian, with Roman Catholic, Church of Sudan, and Pentecostal churches all represented; there was also a small number of Muslims.

Although they came from both rural and urban backgrounds, most had at least some knowledge of cultivation. Many townspeople in south Sudan, whose livelihoods may be based on trading or small business, tend to retain links and land in rural areas, and often supplement their urban-based income with produce from the field. Cultivation, therefore, was not for them an alien concept. However, adapting to a rural life did prove to be more of an economic and social hardship for people from the towns, especially men, because, although they had always cultivated, they were more used to earning a large part of their income from other activities. Men in particular had been involved in activities such as trading, fishing, skills-based work, or government service, which they considered to be more prestigious. Women from towns, who had perhaps more often been responsible for cultivation, had also had their own independent sources of income, from tea-shops or small hotels; Ikafe did not offer them much of a market for their handicrafts.

Similarly, some (but certainly not all) of the pastoralist groups, like the Dinka, Mundari, and a very few Nuer, had traditionally carried out some cultivation, but it was usually done by women, and seen as supplementary to the more important rearing of cattle. A few pastoralists had arrived in Ikafe with good heads of cattle, but the environment was not conducive to cattle-rearing, with little grazing land available, and the area rife with tsetse fly. Adapting to a life where they were entirely dependent on cultivation and forced to settle within a restricted area was extremely difficult, especially for men. At the same time, women had to get used to having their husbands around the home full-time, and to the changes in gender-determined roles and responsibilities which that entailed. Meanwhile, some groups of pastoralists found themselves taking up digging for the very first time in their lives.

As in any society, there was always a good deal of economic stratification across the settlement. People who managed to retain links across the border tended to be better off. Some people had carried significant assets with them from Sudan (including cattle, tools, bicycles, and utensils for small businesses), while others had accumulated things while in Koboko. Those from urban centres were often better educated, and thus in a stronger position to get employment with NGOs. It was these people — inevitably mostly men — who assumed positions of responsibility within the settlement.

A bird's eye view of the settlement

A visitor to the area demarcated as Ikafe would not immediately be aware of entering an area of land occupied by refugees. There were no tents, and no long queues of people waiting for food. Instead, the settlement of Ikafe was made up of small communities, each with 500–600 households, and spaced between 2 and 5 kilometres apart. The huts *(or tukuls)* constructed by the refugees had walls of mud and wood, and thatch roofing. They differed in size and shape according to the particular tribe, but were more or less similar to those of the host population (and those in Sudan). Some families chose to build two or three *tukuls* on the plot of land allocated to them, and the majority put up bathing shelters and dug pit latrines. Many retained a number of larger trees within their compounds, providing much-needed shelter from the scorching sun; flowers and vegetables were planted along the borders. The compounds were cleared of any bush, and swept daily. Two or three main access roads wound through most settlements, with small paths running between the huts.

In fact, the only real visible difference between the settlements of the refugees and those of their Ugandan neighbours was that the homes of the former were in closer proximity to each other, and people did not usually have their kinspeople living next to them. Longer structures, made again from mud and thatch, were erected as churches, with wooden planks serving for pews; and there were similar, larger buildings for schools. Every settlement had its own market, which would consist of at least two or three tea houses, small structures made from grass under which petty commodities were sold, and a space cleared in front for people to sell vegetables, fruit or fish, and for bicycle repairs. In some places cobblers, tailors, blacksmiths, and bicycle repairers would set up shop alongside the food stalls. Wandering through under a late afternoon sun was much like passing through any village in this part of the world at a similar time: women sitting in their compounds sifting through maize, or using traditional grinding stones, children kicking a football made from leaves and twine, men out in the fields or sitting around chatting, and a peaceful buzz of activity around the market place.

Arrival and early settlement (August 1994 — early 1995)

By the time that UNHCR approached Oxfam to take on the management of Ikafe, there was already considerable pressure from the GoU to get started. More refugees were arriving almost daily from areas in the Sudan newly hit by fighting, and the GoU was keen to disband border camps, which now represented an international threat.

A very few refugees had been transferred to Ikafe in May 1994, but it was not until the middle of August that a Memorandum of Understanding (MoU) was signed between UNHCR, the Ministry of Local Government (MoLG), and Oxfam. Oxfam agreed to take on a lead role, with responsibility for water and sanitation, registration, distribution of food and non-food items, community representation, income generation, agriculture, and forestry. Tripartite agreements had already been signed for both the other agencies to be involved. Action Africa in Need (AAIN), a German NGO, was to take on curative health services,[1] and the Jesuit Refugee Service (JRS) was responsible for education. Each had signed separate agreements, so that, although Oxfam had been named as the lead agency, it had no mandate to manage or co-ordinate the activities of the other agencies.

The Memorandum of Understanding established Oxfam as the lead implementing agency in Ikafe, but it was working there only at the invitation of the GoU and UNHCR, and responsible simply for *implementing* a number of activities — not for ensuring other rights, which was the responsibility of the other partners. UNHCR retained overall responsibility for ensuring that the basic needs of all refugees were addressed. This included the protection of vulnerable groups, and overall co-ordination and supervision. They were also initially in charge of registration, and the issuing of contracts to other agencies for road construction and borehole drilling. Food rations were provided in kind by the World Food Programme (WFP). Any appeals from Oxfam to GoU or WFP had to be made through UNHCR.

The Government of Uganda was mandated to ensure the security of the refugees and security within the settlement generally; it was also the GoU which carried out negotiations with local communities for land. Government was also responsible for administration issues (such as the initial refugee registration, movement outside the camp, and the issue of work permits) and for providing overall policy guidance. A Settlement Commandant was seconded to the programme from the government department responsible for refugees, the Ministry of Local Government.

This division of roles and responsibilities often created tension and confusion. Oxfam would be blamed for 'starving' the refugees of food, although it was the responsibility of WFP and UNHCR to ensure timely delivery, and Oxfam could do little other than make appeals on behalf of the refugees. Similarly Oxfam staff would be criticised for not providing blankets or plastic sheets, when it was their role simply to distribute them. Refugees would accuse Oxfam of leaving them exposed to rebel attacks, when it was the responsibility of the GoU to ensure their security. There were similar misunderstandings with the host population, particularly over issues of land rights and access — again issues over which Oxfam never had any control.

Getting started

Oxfam was initially expected to be fully on the ground within just 15 days of signing the MOU. This left very little time to gear up properly, especially for recruitment and planning. Oxfam had all along been begging for more time, but UNHCR was itself under pressure from government to become operational so that the Koboko camps could be cleared. In the end, a two-month incremental take-over was negotiated, so that Oxfam carried out neither the initial registration, nor any of the early surveys. This had a big impact on performance later on, with discrepancies, for example, between agencies (UNHCR, WFP, Oxfam, and AAIN) over the number of refugees actually registered in Ikafe; and prolonged discussion over the actual carrying capacity and resource availability within the gazetted area.

With the pressures to get started, plans and objectives were inevitably produced in a hurry, and there was limited scope to involve other stakeholders and partners. On the other hand, there was a huge amount of energy and excitement surrounding the whole operation, and the Ikafe team received considerable support from a number of sources.

Planning was carried out over a two-week period by a relatively small number of people — something which Oxfam would never have wanted for a programme that sought to involve communities and build up local capacity. But to compensate, a high level of practical and academic expertise was brought in early on to provide some guidance for the programme. A consultant from the Refugee Studies Programme at the University of Oxford, who had spent a lot of time with the Ugandan refugees in Yei District during the 1980s, contributed to discussions at the planning stage, which helped the team to develop the long-term programme. Oxfam offices in Oxford and Kampala gave considerable technical and managerial support, including the secondment of a Gender and Social Development Adviser to the programme for the first six months to guide community development; and two highly qualified accountants for similar periods. Two health advisers gave valuable input to support the move towards a more integrated approach to health-care provision.

From a staff of 3 to 63

Recruiting a huge number of qualified staff at very short notice was not easy. Oxfam wanted people who would bring with them experience and expertise, but it was also aware of the political and economic benefits of offering opportunities locally. Having been refugees themselves, the local population had their own skills to offer, in particular a working knowledge of 'Juba Arabic', the common language for many of the southern Sudanese; and a good understanding of the refugee population and of refugee life.

In the end, with the pressures of time, a few drivers, distribution workers, and technical staff were imported from other Oxfam relief programmes to get operations off the ground. They brought with them experience of Oxfam's ways of working. At the same time, recruitment went on locally, especially for the lower management positions. By late 1994, over 60 staff had been taken on board. One week was set aside to give all staff a basic training in gender-fair ways of working, and an introduction to Oxfam's values and practices.

Within six weeks of the signing of the agreement, recruitment and training were almost complete (with the exception of a few positions which were still proving difficult to fill in the middle of 1995), and Oxfam was in a position to take on full camp management. Bush was cleared, water tanks set up, and tents erected. These would serve as home and office space for well over a year. The Ikafe programme was finally coming to life.

'Dumped in the bush'

By December 1994, the Ikafe settlement was already filling up, with some 22,383 refugees (5,632 households) officially registered. But there was still pressure from government officials to take on more refugees, because they were keen to empty the border camps in Koboko. UNHCR did not want to jeopardise the offer of land, with the opportunity it created to reduce the high costs of supporting Sudanese refugees in care-and-maintenance camps. Over 30,000 refugees remained in the Koboko camps, and more were expected. Already up to 500 refugees had begun crossing from Sudan every day in the wake of more fighting on the border north-east of Ikafe. Some of these were absorbed straight into the settlement.

right Arriving refugees off-load their possessions from a truck.

Oxfam/Jenny Matthews

Oxfam was concerned to address the basic rights of any refugees transferred, but seriously questioned its ability to do so, without adequate infrastructure in place. The Project Manager recalls:

> ‘ Some people were being literally dumped in the bush, or on the roadside somewhere near Yumbe town, and expected to set up home. We were receiving up to 1,000 people a day. They were given some non-food items — plastic sheets, pangas [machetes], sickles and some kitchen utensils — but these sometimes ran short. ’

Sara T., a refugee in central Ikafe, described what it felt like arriving in Ikafe:

> ‘ Everything took a long time at the Koboko end, and our truck did not arrive in Aringa until 4 pm. Then we all had to be registered. After two hours we began to look at where we'd come to. It was thick with bush, with tiny posts marking out the different plots. It was too late to give out our plots or non-food items that night, so we all slept together out in the open. I felt very lonely, and Sudan seemed to be a long way off. ’

Access to the settlement was extremely poor, with the very few roads poorly maintained and water-logged during the wet season. Natural sources of water were a consistent problem. Only 11 boreholes existed in the whole area of Ikafe, and in these the water-table fluctuated dramatically. Monica P. and Esther D. recalled some of the early days:

> ‘ Some were dumped without shelter and water. In Loblucho [north Ikafe], the most acute problem was water and shelter. There was no grass, and the place was completely dry. People used to queue at the nationals' boreholes throughout the night. This led to fights with nationals, between the refugees themselves and within the home. There was little cooking or bathing. We had to walk five kilometres to the Kochi river for water. ’

Staff had not had time to build trust with the community, and Oxfam took the brunt of their frustrations, as a Public Health Promoter recalls:

> ‘ They would come in and storm the compounds, demanding food or water. Imagine: the whole Point [a group of 500–600 households] — women, children, men, all armed with pangas, speaking in chorus. One time in Iyete when [the Distribution Co-ordinator] was not around, they were so angry that they looted all the sanitation tools. All the compounds were affected. One time they took me by force down to their Point to taste the bitter food they were having to eat. Another time they made [my colleague] swallow the dirty water they were being forced to drink. ’

Refugees felt that Oxfam was not doing enough to respond to their basic needs, while Oxfam on the other hand was struggling to persuade UNHCR to delay transfers in order to ensure that adequate infrastructure was in place for the 60,000 who had been planned for. The Project Manager recalled:

❦ There was already strain on the existing boreholes when the first 2,100 refugees arrived, and the drilling companies were having problems. For our part, we did not want refugees transferred to yet another transit area before being allocated their plots for settlement, when they had already moved around so much. ❞

It was particularly important that boreholes were drilled and access roads completed, so that food or tankered water would be able to reach the occupied parts of the settlement. The series of requests created tensions in the relationship between Oxfam and UNHCR in Kampala, and in December 1994 Oxfam was given notice that it would be replaced in early 1995, on account of 'slow progress'. However, the threat was withdrawn when the issue was taken up by Oxfam in Geneva.

How many refugees could Ikafe take?

Apart from the inadequacy of the infrastructure, there was the question of the availability of land. Oxfam questioned the degree to which surveys carried out by UNHCR and MoLG had taken into account the geology of the area, and in particular the huge variations in soil quality which would affect the productive capacity of the land. In the view of their own surveyors, were UNHCR to insist on a population of 60,000, a number of households would never be able to reach self-sufficiency. (The carrying capacity of Ikafe had originally been estimated at 100,000, but this figure was reduced after more detailed surveys to 60,000. Oxfam, however, continued to question whether Ikafe would ever be able to sustain more than 42,000 refugees.)

Despite Oxfam's reservations, transfers went ahead regardless. In January 1995, 15,223 people were received, at an average of 700 per day. As a result, it was necessary to put some people into temporary transit areas, something which Oxfam had all along struggled to avoid, because basic facilities were simply not adequate. Borehole drilling was incomplete in many of the places where refugees were supposed to settle, and it was not always logistically feasible to deliver water by tanker. Roads were still very poor, and drivers and other resources already fully stretched.

As refugees were gradually settled, the allocation of agricultural land was delayed, because there was no agreement on the size of plots that each family should receive, and how many people the gazetted area of Ikafe could sustain.

As a result, seeds and tools were distributed, but families were restricted to sowing on the areas around their *tukuls* on the small pieces of land given for residential purposes. Later on, as disputes continued, small plots of agricultural land, ranging between 0.2 and 0.4 hectares, were given out temporarily in the main part of Ikafe which had been settled first; the plots were allocated per family rather than per capita, in order that households could catch the planting season.

The disputes over Ikafe's carrying capacity, and negotiations about plans to transfer the remaining refugees, were to continue right through until the end of 1996. The high level of uncertainty over refugee numbers made planning very difficult. The Project Manager again explains some of the other shorter-term implications:

> ❨ We had difficulties with budgeting. It made a big difference if we were planning for 60,000 refugees or just 45,000. It was also hard deciding how to go ahead. In [the later extensions to Ikafe], for example, we prepared for arrivals months before the transfer dates were actually confirmed. Roads were opened up and a physical land survey carried out, so the sites would be ready this time if the transfers came. It was a gamble, but one that paid off, because refugees in those areas were much better received. ❩

Meanwhile, tensions in relations with the local population increased from the middle of 1995, because of pressures on local water resources, especially where refugees had been transferred too early. The Aringa youth and local politicians, in particular, had very high expectations of compensation in the form of infrastructure and employment. Managers held meetings to try to resolve issues of land compensation or violation of sacred areas, while field workers struggled to find solutions to the growing animosity between refugees and their hosts. As a staff member recalled: *'We held meeting after meeting between nationals and refugees, trying to get them to share resources, but they could never appreciate it, because of course they did not have enough facilities themselves.'*

The settlement takes shape (1995 — June 96)

Despite the problems, people gradually did begin to settle. Small communities were established, consisting of between 500 and 600 households, known as a 'Point'. There were 22 Points in main Ikafe. Each had a small school, an area set aside for a market and for sports activities, and places demarcated for churches or mosques. Burial sites were not demarcated unless specifically requested, because people preferred to bury their dead with them on their compounds. Each household was given a residential plot measuring 20m x 30m, on which they were expected to construct a home.

Ikafe settlement structure

Zone:	4 in main Ikafe
Point:	500–600 households
Village:	3–4 per Point
Block:	24 households

Everyday activities began to take shape. Markets were established at an incredible speed, small teashops and 'hotels' began to operate, and women throughout the settlement were not slow to start up their brewing businesses. Men in particular used bicycles to bring small commodities and dried fish in from Koboko or Arua. People grew vegetables and cowpeas around their homes. The small mud and thatch huts known as *tukuls* were quickly established, and compounds were cleared and swept clean. Some began to dig pit latrines and put up bathing shelters. The individual Points began to take the shape of tight communities, with people living in closer proximity than they were accustomed to in Sudan, but using the opportunity that this created to form relationships with neighbours who were often people from a different tribe.

Structures for churches and mosques were put up within a matter of weeks; and women's groups which had started up in Koboko under the auspices of the churches were re-formed and began to meet regularly, mostly to discuss income generation and self-help initiatives. The younger people formed committees, cleared fields for football or volleyball, and planted trees around the sites in return for sports equipment. As one of the refugee extension staff remembers:

> ❪ Very early on, some of the youths began to build houses for the vulnerable people. Many of the Points quickly formed water committees, and people we called water-source caretakers were selected to do things like clean around the boreholes, and check times for use. ❫

Schools began to operate, and children who were being educated in Koboko and Arua were transferred to Ikafe, so that they could be with their families. People attended health centres, and traditional birth attendants began to supervise deliveries within the Points.

Weddings became more frequent, and Christmas and Easter celebrations were held all over the settlement. The Project Manager recalled:

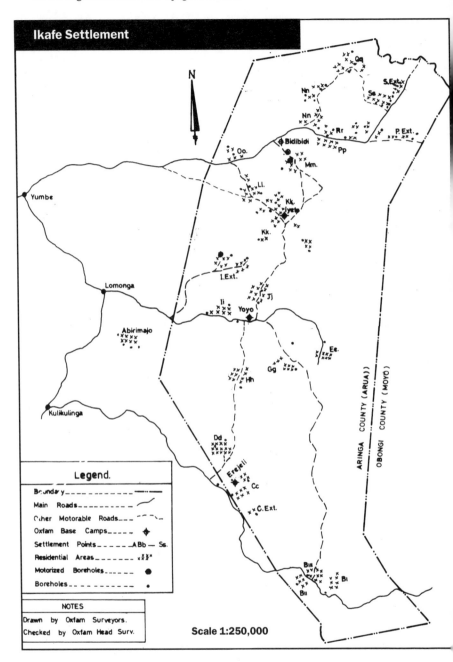

Ikafe Settlement

N

Yumbe

Lomonga

Abirimajo

Kulikulinga

Oo.

Bidibidi

Mm.

Ll.

Kk.
Iyete

Kk.

I.Ext.

Ii
Yoyo

Jj

Ee.

Gg

Hh

Dd

Erejeli
Cc

C.Ext.

Qq

S.Ext.

Ss

Nn

Nn

Rr

P. Ext.

Pp

Bil

Bi

Bll

ARINGA COUNTY (ARUA))

OBONGI COUNTY (MOYO)

Legend.

Boundary _ _ _ _ _ _ _ _ _ _

Main Roads _ _ _ _ _ _ _ _

Other Motorable Roads _ _ _

Oxfam Base Camps _ _ _ _ _

Settlement Points _ _ _ _ _ _ A Bb — Ss.

Residential Areas _ _ _ _ _ _ _

Motorized Boreholes _ _ _ _ _

Boreholes _ _ _ _ _ _ _ _ _

NOTES

Drawn by Oxfam Surveyors.
Checked by Oxfam Head Surv.

Scale 1:250,000

❛ Within six months, the refugees had achieved a considerable amount. People had vegetable gardens, after the first year almost every home had a few chickens, and quite a few had goats. By the end of 1995, many refugees bought clothing for the Christmas celebrations from sales of their vegetables or chickens. We were invited to a number of marriage ceremonies. ❜

Many of the refugees' initial reservations about moving to Ikafe — because of its remote location and the fact that they had already established lives in Koboko — were gradually dispelled as the settlement began to take shape, and — for people from rural areas at least — it began to resemble a life that was familiar to them from the Sudan.

Ikafe expands

With a population of 46,267 (12,721 households) by March 1995, there was still pressure to take on more refugees, and the government began discussions about two new settlement areas. The first, Northern Extension, lay to the north of Ikafe, very close to the Sudan border, and the second, Imvepi, fell in a neighbouring county, to the south-west.

In November 1995, a census was carried out in the main (original) part of Ikafe, and the total settled population was found to stand at just 32,000. Some 14,000 refugees had obviously managed to get themselves registered twice, a familiar state of affairs in refugee situations, where people are keen to take advantage of the packages provided on arrival, including high-value items like plastic sheets or blankets.

The reduced population was a good thing in some respects, because Oxfam had all along been voicing concerns about the carrying capacity of the land. There was now a possibility of allocating larger tracts of land to refugees. Yet there was persistent pressure to absorb some of the remaining people from the Koboko camps, and, with such a dramatically reduced population, Ikafe was the obvious choice. In fact, in terms of resolving the disputes over the numbers the settlement could sustain, the census had not helped the agencies concerned to get any closer to an agreement, and UNHCR, Oxfam, and the government were still at loggerheads in the middle of 1996.

While the issue of population size for main Ikafe remained unresolved, the area of Northern Extension was occupied by around 11,000 refugees from late 1995, and just over 9,000 people were transferred to ten Points in Imvepi between January and May 1996. By mid-1996, the total population of both settlements was 55,162, or 19,929 households. Disputes over the carrying capacity of the new sites re-emerged, but Oxfam this time carried out its own

above A church-based women's group in Ikafe. Structures for churches and mosques were built within weeks of the refugees' arrival.

right Markets flourished in the early months.

survey in advance, which revealed a high density of local settlement, and reduced the estimated size of population that Northern Extension could absorb by 4,500. Because surveys had been done in advance, Oxfam was able to negotiate much better terms for the new areas, with a per capita land allocation of 0.33 hectares in Northern Extension and between 0.2 and 0.33 per person in Imvepi. Around this time, the original allocations to families in main Ikafe were supplemented to 0.4 hectares wherever possible, but the allocation was still made on a family basis, which was never considered adequate by any of the parties involved.

The settlement process in Northern Extension and Imvepi went much more smoothly, largely because Oxfam was able to draw on lessons from the initial Ikafe transfers, and had had time to prepare. Land was surveyed and the carrying capacity assessed well in advance. No one was transferred to either of the sites until staff, resources, and infrastructure were in place, and Oxfam was able to insist on refugees being directly settled, rather than being moved to another transit site. In fact, implementation for Imvepi was delayed, precisely because funding and resources were insufficient to ensure adequate infrastructure.

Settlement in Ikafe/Imvepi

Zone	Point	Village	Block	Household	Population
North	10	96	322	7,385	19,468
Central	7	36	155	3,555	9,432
South	5	25	111	2,856	613
N.Ext.	12	43	159	3,644	10,639
Imvepi	10	32	110	2.549	9,310
Total	44	232	857	19,929	55,162

Organisational constraints

It soon became apparent that Oxfam needed to have more control over some of the other sectors which had initially been the responsibility of UNHCR, or contracted out by them to other agencies and NGOs, such as CARE. Being responsible for road construction, for example, would avoid delays in tankering and the problems of reaching the more remote locations for food distribution. With its own surveyors, Oxfam could ensure that plot demarcation was properly supervised. It would also have benefited from having more control over contracts for borehole drilling, so that sites could

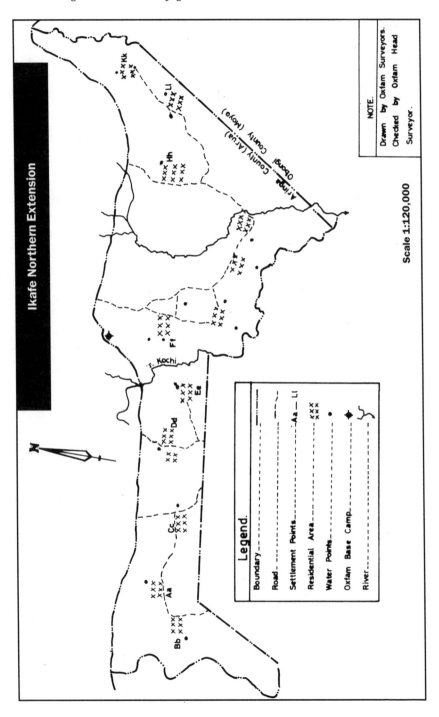

Ikafe Northern Extension

Scale 1:120,000

NOTE.
Drawn by Oxfam Surveyors.
Checked by Oxfam Head
Surveyor.

Legend.

Boundary	
Road	
Settlement Points	Aa — Ll
Residential Area	xxx
Water Points	●
Oxfam Base Camp	✦
River	

Arrupi County (Arua)
Obongi County (Moyo)

Kochi

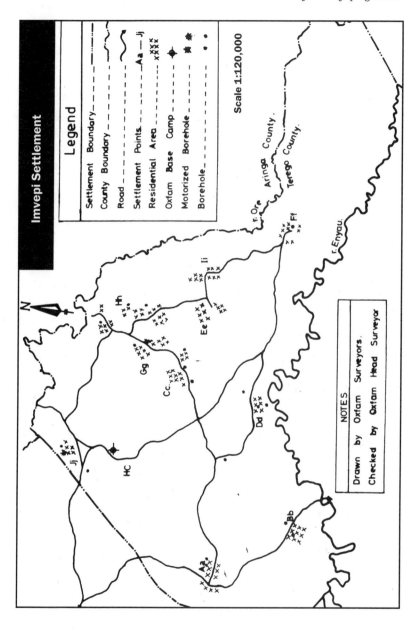

Imvepi Settlement

Legend

Settlement Boundary	— · · — · ·
County Boundary	— — — —
Road	— — —
Settlement Points	Aa — Jj
Residential Area	xxx
Oxfam Base Camp	✦
Motorized Borehole	✿
Borehole	•

Scale 1:120,000

r. Ora
Aringa County.
Terego County.
r. Enyau.

Ff

Ii

Hh

Ee

Gg

Cc

Dd

Jj

HC

Bb

NOTES

Drawn by Oxfam Surveyors.
Checked by Oxfam Head Surveyor

have been better prioritised. By early 1996, Oxfam had taken over both surveying and road construction; and had also begun preparations for a health programme in Imvepi. This would provide the chance to adopt a truly integrated approach to the settlement process.

The physical area which Oxfam now managed was huge, stretching over 50 km from north to south direct; but, since access roads were never completed, it would take well over an hour and a half to reach some parts of Imvepi from the main office compound. Routes were often extremely difficult or impassable, and it was not unusual to spend 2–3 hours travelling to one location. The entire surface area of Ikafe alone was over 42,000 hectares. Constructing *tukuls* for each of the 150 members of staff was in itself a massive project. To ease operations, the settlement was split into four separate zones, with Imvepi forming the fifth. 'Bidibidi' (a local hunting term meaning 'resting place') housed the central offices, stores, and main workshop to the north of the settlement, while smaller compounds for staff were established in each of the other zones.

The sheer size of the programme — in terms of the physical area, as well as material resources and staff numbers — remained a hurdle. Holding a meeting for extension staff, for example, was a taxing logistical exercise, and monitoring operations on such a huge scale always a challenge. This became considerably worse when insecurity limited travel still further.

Trying to build capacity at high speed

Apart from all the physical work, such as constructing roads and schools, and tankering water, Oxfam also had to put in place a framework for building community capacity. Establishing representative structures which would facilitate channels for communication from the level of the individual household right up to the agency staff was always a priority. A comprehensive structure was established from Block level through to Zonal level, with elected officers who had various responsibilities.

The structure mirrored the Ugandan local administration, and it was hoped that this would stimulate better integration between the two communities. Point leaders would become the key link between Oxfam and the community, while traditional representatives from the Ugandan and Sudanese communities, such as chiefs, elders, and other relevant leaders, would be able to meet independently of Oxfam to sort out other issues such as law and order, and gain a better understanding of their respective social and cultural expectations. None of these leaders was paid, in the hope that this would build up a sense of community responsibility.

It soon became apparent, however, that there was an urgent need to push forward activities at the community level. Digging a pit latrine, for example, was hardly a priority for a single-headed household struggling to put up a hut and clear some agricultural land, but it was essential in order to avoid an outbreak of disease. Promoting the benefits of environmental hygiene needed more intensive 'extension' work. It was unlikely that a Point Leader would find the time to visit agricultural plots individually to discuss the merits of improved agro-forestry practice. The general needs of the community were getting forgotten as people rushed to clear land and establish homes for themselves. Relatives who would normally be responsible for the disadvantaged, especially people with disabilities and the very old, were understandably putting the needs of their immediate families first. Oxfam found that at times it needed key people on whom it could rely to supply information or to supervise activities. So in early 1995, over 80 refugee extension workers were taken on to support work on public health, agro-forestry, and community development for a period of one year, to help to get programmes on the right track.

Ikafe begins to flower

The harvest for the first cropping season falls in Ikafe between October and December. For many of the refugees settled in mid- and late 1994, this 1995 harvest marked the beginning of their moving towards a semblance of normality. As Martina S., one of the very first Ikafe settlers, explained:

> ❡ Although people had not wanted to come from Koboko, they later settled and were happy after cultivating in the first year. The yield was very good, which pleased them. All settlers were happy, and had planned for their future ... People lost thinking about the Sudan. Their main aim was to build up a good state of living. ❡

John and Charles D. tell a similar story:

> ❡ [By early 1996] most of us had got a good yield and enough to eat, as well as for sale. Everybody was happy. Some planned to make businesses, while others started to build their permanent houses in the settlement ... Settlers were happy and had planned for their future and better living. ❡

Looking to the future was particularly important for people who had been living for years under a cloud of uncertainty. As Sebit C. put it: *'We planted, things grew, and we all had a good yield ... We all felt positive.'* Over the years, people had lost assets through looting, distress sales, and the need to keep moving from one place to another, as areas in Sudan variously became safe or unsafe zones to inhabit. After a good harvest, they felt they had a chance to

27

Oxfam/Jenny Matthews

begin to build things up again. James M. recalled: *'The first year we cultivated
sweet potatoes, simsim, and serena, and the harvest was good. I bought a bicycle, a
radio cassette, and new shoes — all from the field.'* Mary Z. added: *'When my
brother died, I performed the last funeral rites from my garden — that was just from
the first season.'*

Walking through the settlements in main Ikafe by the end of 1995, it was
difficult to believe that the communities had been in place for hardly a year.
Small trading centres were established in most Points, alongside tea-shops
and bicycle repairers, while larger markets which attracted local Ugandans
developed in each of the zones. Compounds were well swept, and many were
awash with colour from flowers brought from Sudan. Some began to invest in

better housing, using sun-dried bricks, which increased the sense of permanency; fruit trees were planted and vegetables flourished in the kitchen gardens. Music and life began to sing out from within the *tukuls*.

Return to emergency programming (June 1996 — June 1997)

But this semblance of normality was not to last for long. For Oxfam the environment had never been really stable — certainly not enough to plan with a clear vision of the future. There were always problems: pressures of time, lack of clarity over objectives, and uncertainty about how many refugees could be expected. For the refugees, though, it was April 1996 which marked the end of the brief interlude when it had been possible to feel something akin to being settled.

In mid-April, forces of the rebel West Nile Bank Front (WNBF) began crossing from hideouts in Sudan in the wake of Presidential elections — the first to be held in Uganda for many years. The group was made up of supporters of Idi Amin, led by one of his former generals, Juma Oris. Their aim initially was to disrupt the Presidential elections, and to stage a coup if Museveni won. A second agenda was to destabilise the north more generally, to disrupt the support allegedly given by Ugandan government military forces to the SPLA. It was claimed that the WNBF rebels were armed and supported by the Government of Sudan, although a good number had carried their guns from Uganda with them into exile in the early 1980s. The group had had bases in Sudan and former Zaire since the time when people fled there as refugees following Amin's overthrow. They had also retained a strong support base within Arua District, mostly among people who considered themselves to have been marginalised economically since Amin was overthrown. A significant proportion of the rebels were reportedly from within Aringa county, so it was inevitably through Aringa, where they had relatives and therefore easy cover and good networks, that they decided to cross.

The rebels were heavily armed. When they targeted Oxfam vehicles, it was initially to commandeer them to carry arms or personnel. Three were ambushed in separate incidents on the morning of 18 April 1996, two from within Imvepi, and staff were made to walk at gunpoint for over two hours. At the same time, a Dinka refugee was brutally hacked to death just outside the settlement. The Dinka are commonly associated with the SPLA, and the incident was interpreted by refugees as a firm indication from rebel Ugandan factions that the SPLA were to be targeted. This sent a wave of fear throughout both settlements, because it was commonly assumed (even if unproved) that the camps harboured SPLA supporters, which meant that all refugees were potential political targets. Fears grew as Sudanese bomber planes were spotted passing over Ikafe.

'We have nowhere to run to'

Life for the refugees deteriorated rapidly from June 1996. As rebels passed through the settlement, communities were attacked, homes burned, women raped, and thousands of refugees robbed. By the end of June, over 7,000 people from south Ikafe were displaced to other parts of the settlement. This happened at a critical point in the cultivation season, and thousands lost the crops they had worked so hard for, because they were unable to harvest.

Hardened perhaps by many years of civil strife, however, the refugees in Ikafe proved that they were not so easily chased away. Although a sense of fear pervaded the settlements, by August 1996 many of those who had been forced to flee were persuaded to return to their homes and fields in order to dig for the second planting season. Markets continued to function and grow. A good number of the refugees showed that they had begun to see Ikafe as a better option than the overcrowded transits of Koboko, and they were determined to try to hang on to what the settlement had to offer.

Oxfam becomes a target

The agencies involved in the Ikafe programme had themselves also become targets. As groups of WNBF rebels pushed forward, they were split into potentially more dangerous, smaller groups of four or five well-armed men, short of food and cash. Roads became unsafe for travel, with frequent ambushes. Staff were held up and forced to hand over money, radios or clothing. Movement was severely restricted, and with it Oxfam's ability to sustain programming.

This was all combined with growing anger and threats from local politicians and youth — many of whom, it later turned out, had rebel connections. 'Hit lists' were circulated, with the names of staff who, the local Aringa felt, had been unfairly employed, thus cheating them of jobs. Staff became increasingly uneasy. Vehicles were held on a couple of occasions, and Oxfam was forced to pay ransoms for their release. Several very tense meetings were held with local representatives, in which Oxfam was at the sharp end of accusations. The anger and frustrations culminated in an armed attack on the Bidibidi compound in mid-June. Gunfire resounded through the compound for an hour and a half, and stick grenades were later found in the office block. Fortunately there were no casualties, although bullets went straight through people's houses and tents, some landing on the beds under which staff were taking cover. The attack was more or less repulsed by police, but it was decided to evacuate most staff, for fear of a second onslaught, and to give them a much-needed break. Only a very few members of staff stayed on in Bidibidi, in order to monitor the situation and make proper plans should a full withdrawal become necessary.

It was a major concern that the refugees should not feel abandoned, and as such it was essential that managers met with leaders to reassure them, and to discuss how communication could be maintained should Oxfam be forced to leave. Withdrawal would involve a massive logistical exercise. With a fleet of over 30 vehicles, and two warehouses full of water equipment, construction materials, and all the food and non-food items donated by UNHCR and WFP, withdrawal was always a last option. Yet, however much Oxfam felt a responsibility to the refugees for their welfare, it was obliged to put the safety of staff first. It was an extremely difficult situation.

Events, however, took another turn just two days later, when Bidibidi again became a battlefield. This time the attackers were stronger and less successfully repulsed. A number of homes were looted, and shots were fired inside *tukuls* where some staff were hiding. The remaining staff left that morning in a huge convoy of vehicles, without a second chance to consult refugees, along a route that had been ambushed an hour before.

The entire staff then sat frustrated in Arua Town, some 70 km from Ikafe, for almost a month, before beginning a phased return to Bidibidi. There were still reports of rebel activity throughout the south and central parts of Ikafe, and, as a result, staff and many activities other than humanitarian relief were excluded from a large part of the settlement.

In mid-September 1996 the Settlement Commandant, who was a senior officer in the MoLG, seconded to the Ikafe programme as the primary government representative, was killed in an ambush at Yoyo in the central zone of Ikafe. He had always been a great source of support to the programme, and a friend to many Oxfam colleagues. He was a courageous man who had worked hard to support the refugees and to improve relationships between different groups and officials. The ambush that killed him marked a further deterioration of security in the whole area. From this time on, as rebel bases in Sudan and Zaire were systematically squeezed by the advances of the SPLA and the forces of the Democratic Republic of Congo respectively, the WNBF was pushed back into Uganda, and there followed a series of increasingly more desperate attacks and general looting, which disorganised the whole area.

With rebels apparently closing in on Bidibidi, and attacks on the compound and staff of a neighbouring camp, Oxfam was again forced to evacuate. It was the end of Oxfam's permanent presence in Ikafe settlement. Skeleton operations continued, but refugees were already widely dispersed. Shortly afterwards, the UN declared the whole area to be under Phase 4 of their Security Guidelines, which allows for the continuation of life-saving activities only, with minimal staff presence. The final phase — 5 — would have meant evacuating all staff from Arua District.

October 1996 — February 1997

For staff from Oxfam and the other agencies, moving away from the danger zones when things deteriorated was a relatively easy process. For refugees, it was a different story. From September 1996, when the new group of rebels entered the area, refugees throughout both settlements began to lose hope of a stable future in Arua District. They were thinking only of staying alive, safeguarding what property remained, and educating their children.

Attacks continued systematically for the remainder of the year, and into 1997, as gradually more and more of the population, from the extreme south through the central areas and on to Northern Extension, were displaced — a pattern that was repeated in Imvepi. Testimonies taken at the time point to the grim reality. Martin I., for example, remembers:

> ❧ All my properties were burned; my bicycle and two radio cassettes all looted. My madam left with only the dressing on her body ... no shelter ... raping was mostly to young girls, even pregnant women. Pangas [machetes] were used, and some people were hurt. All the five villages were burned, with exception of two Dinka Blocks [about 48 houses]. ❧

Gordon C. paints a similar picture:

> ❧ My sister's daughter of 16 years was taken and held for two days; she was repeatedly raped. Two of my cousin-brothers were cut with pangas, one on the ankle and arm. People were given matches to burn their own homes. They were told to go straight to Sudan, not to delay by going first to Bidibidi. ❧

For women, the risks were greater, especially if they were alone — as Cecilia S., a single woman from Ikafe, attests:

> ❧ After the first attack, I moved from Point to Point; I was afraid to sleep in my own home. Sometimes I slept in the bush, sometimes with friends. I appealed to UNHCR for protection, but there was no action. My mind was badly disturbed. I had most of my things looted in the first attack. Then when the rebels burned Point J, I lost whatever was

remaining. They told us that they didn't want to see anyone left in the camps ... I feared in my heart that I [would] be killed. 🥢

The refugees were legally supposed to stay within the areas assigned and 'gazetted' by the government. But as one attack followed another, literally thousands chose to de-camp to Yumbe Town, which was about 20 km from Bidibidi in the north of Ikafe, but closer to the central part of the settlement. Others returned to the town of Koboko. People genuinely feared for their lives, and felt that they would be better protected in a Ugandan town, where they would be less of a target than if they were isolated in the bush. This was particularly the case in Koboko, where many of the refugees shared a common language with their (Ugandan) Kakwa hosts; it was also much closer to Sudan. Many hoped that, by moving out of the settlement, they would force the government and UNHCR to take the issue of security more seriously.

Addressing their basic needs outside the settlement area, especially for food, water and shelter, was a new challenge for Oxfam. The government was reluctant to allow services like food distribution outside the demarcated settlement area; the route to fetch water for tankering was extremely insecure; and there were very few plastic sheets or jerry cans available for the hundreds of families who had lost all their property. There were also serious implications for health and social stability, in a community that was so heavily traumatised. Interviewed during that time, Alice P. complained:

🥢 Women are delivering in the bush; young children are dying. When people die outside the gazetted area [of Ikafe], there is nowhere to bury them. Some new-borns have been born and buried under trees. Where is the dignity in that? 🥢

After a couple of months, refugees were persuaded to return to a large temporary 'transit' camp established close to a military base at Bidibidi. A 'transit' represents everything that the concept of Ikafe had sought to avoid: rows of make-shift shelters constructed from plastic sheets or grass, crowded into a tiny area; nothing like the compounds that had characterised Ikafe; no room to cultivate or even to plant just a few vegetables in order to supplement the diet, or to tide things over when food supplies were short. The refugees had been thrown back into a situation where they were once again entirely dependent on external assistance, with all the health risks that are created by heavily over-crowded camp situations.

The transit around Bidibidi expanded systematically as more and more settlements were attacked, and by February 1997 there were more than 32,000 refugees sheltering there in extremely basic conditions. The pattern was repeated in Imvepi, where there was the added problem of having to tanker water to refugees. This became considerably more difficult after one of the hired trucks tankering in Imvepi was burned by rebels in November 1996, and local transporters understandably became reluctant to operate in such an insecure situation.

Things finally came to a head for refugees from main Ikafe in late February 1997, with an armed rebel attack on the security forces based at Bidibidi. Seven refugees who were staying in the temporary transit around the compound were shot dead in crossfire. This resulted in mass evacuation to nearby towns. In Imvepi, a similar process was prompted by armed looting within the transit, when six young men had their ears cut off with machetes. Following SPLA advances in early March 1997, many of the original inhabitants of Ikafe returned to Sudan. Most of the others decamped to Yumbe or Koboko towns. A verification carried out in Koboko and Yumbe towns, and in Imvepi during April, registered 30,523 refugees (9,958 households) who had formerly been residents of Ikafe or Imvepi.

Trying to hold things together

Oxfam could do little more during this period than react to an ever-changing situation. Longer-term objectives were put aside as pressures mounted for life-saving activities. Even these were difficult to maintain, as trucks carrying food were burned, and water tankers attacked both near Yumbe and in Imvepi. There was also a serious shortage of anything to offer as shelter for the displaced refugees, some of whom did not even have cooking pots or jerry cans with them. It was a struggle trying to address even basic needs, when refugees were so mobile and no one knew what the next day would bring. The following extract from a report in September 1996 illustrates the reality for much of that year:

> ❢ Refugees refused to produce ration cards, claiming that they had not had time to collect them ... A 15-day ration only was given, in fear of probable looting. Imvepi urgently needs food, but travel restrictions have so far prevented this ... Schools are too small and men are sleeping outside ... There is a serious lack of blankets and plastic sheeting. Cooking utensils and jerry cans are in short supply, as are tools for constructing communal pit latrines ... Quantities required may reduce or increase, depending on the security situation and whether displaced people decide to return home. ❢

The priority for Oxfam throughout this period was to address the basic needs (food, shelter, water, and sanitation) of displaced refugees. Where it seemed that their rights were being compromised, appeals were made to UNHCR and government, especially to provide non-food items and to improve security. This at times soured relations between Oxfam and the other two signatories to the MoU. In early 1997, JRS reluctantly decided to abandon operations in the District because of the security risks, and Oxfam was persuaded to take on a caretaker role for education, because it continued to be such a priority for the refugees.

Food was a major issue. Delivery of food supplies was consistently delayed, mostly because of insecurity on the route from Kampala, at a time when refugees' assets and hence their coping abilities were at an all-time low. People displaced in Yumbe had no other source of food or income. Most could not return to their fields to cultivate or harvest. The majority had lost all their property and savings, and with them any other means of livelihood; opportunities for piece-rate work were extremely limited. Malnutrition became evident, especially among children, with many mothers unable to produce milk to breastfeed, and older children persistently hit by disease in the heavily overcrowded transits. As Sarah D., displaced in Yumbe, explained at the time:

> ❝ Everyone is becoming too weak; we have been walking up and down, moving from Point to Point, then to Yumbe, now here in Bidibidi. We have had no food for three weeks now. God blessed me with this child six weeks ago, but she's not growing. I have no milk, because I have no food, and now I fear I'll lose her. ❞

Oxfam struggled to maintain food delivery, by getting refugee leaders to handle the process of distribution; this involved lengthy discussions with WFP, who were understandably concerned that food would be lost. Later on, government was persuaded to allow food delivery on humanitarian grounds outside the settlement areas in Koboko and Yumbe towns. But beyond this, there was little that anyone could do.

Throughout the period from mid-September 1996 to late April 1997, Oxfam was hardly on the ground. A core team of 20 local staff operated from Yumbe town, with managers making rushed trips along unsafe roads in and out of the area. Otherwise, it was the few refugees in higher-up positions who proved to be a key asset in keeping operations going. In April, a dedicated driver was shot while tankering water to displaced people in Yumbe. He sadly later died. Quite incredibly, this was the only serious casualty to an Oxfam staff member during a year of persistent insecurity.

Scaling down
In addition to all the physical problems of trying to respond to an ever-deteriorating situation, the programme was faced throughout the year of 1996 with severe financial constraints. The budget was re-written a total of thirteen

times, and a similar pattern re-emerged in 1997. Planned activities were constantly thwarted, either by lack of funds or because of insecurity. It was difficult to raise funds at all, and donors who had already made commitments were reluctant to throw money down an apparently bottomless pit.

Staff morale reached an all-time low. As the year went on, the job losses that had been threatened throughout the year finally became a reality — at a time when staff were already at a low ebb because of all that had happened to the Ikafe programme. With the constraints of having to plan and manage field activities that were almost impossible to visit, the laying off of staff served only to reduce morale still further. It was not helped by the prolonged sickness and death of nine colleagues between 1996 and 1997.

Ikafe is closed

By April 1997, over half of the refugee population had returned to Sudan in what many saw as forced repatriation — forced because of the failure to secure a safe environment for refugees. Their return was encouraged by the presence of SPLA officials within the District,who were reported to be actively seeking military recruits, and offering free transport to help others return to Sudan. (The SPLA, and its various supporters, had an interest in encouraging people to return, as it would appear to re-affirm that peace had really come to the liberated areas.) Ikafe was considered too insecure and anyway too large, given the diminished size of its population, so in June 1997, UNHCR and government made the decision to close it. The remaining refugees (some of whom were new arrivals from the border areas, fleeing from drought) were transferred to the settlement in Imvepi and the neighbouring Rhino Camp in July 1997.

A new start in Imvepi

Oxfam is still (May 1998) operating in Imvepi, with a much smaller programme for around 13,500 refugees. They are highly mobile, and numbers are difficult to monitor. Many of the revised systems have been transferred from Ikafe and the lessons applied, and staff have slowly begun to win back their confidence in the original vision of the Ikafe settlement. They have invested a remarkable amount of energy to get Imvepi back on its feet. It has seemed much more difficult for the refugees to start again. For some, this is the third time they have been asked to construct a home and build a new life.

Yet many show an extraordinary tenacity. A few months on, a visit round the settlement finds fields green with crops, schools operating under trees and makeshift shelters, and homes beginning to be built. But the situation remains turbulent. As this book was being written in late October 1997, rebels again entered the settlement. Refugees' houses in one Point were looted; 18 people were abducted at gunpoint, mostly young girls and boys; several were raped; they were later rescued, although one lost her life in the crossfire. Over half the population decamped again to a heavily overcrowded transit area, and Oxfam was once again obliged to plan how to provide for their various needs in the very short term. At the same time, activities in Imvepi are again beset by the funding problems that plagued the Ikafe programme for the last two years. Forward planning is almost impossible, because nobody knows what the future has in store.

Oxfam/Jenny Matthews

An 'enabling environment'? 2

This chapter considers some of the social, political, and physical factors which defined the context in which the Ikafe programme operated. It begins by looking at the refugees' subjective perspectives. As much of the third chapter will show, it was often emotional and personal factors which affected the degree to which the programme's planned activities succeeded.

The second part of this chapter considers the host community, which had its own priorities and concerns, creating another set of problems. The local context ultimately plays a large part in determining the success or failure of a refugee programme — as the Ikafe programme has painfully shown. To be sustainable, the refugee community needed to be closely integrated into the social, legal, political, and economic systems of the host community; and integration would be possible only if the local population was committed to it. The chapter then moves on to consider the physical environment of the programme: the location of the settlement itself, the geo-physical and economic opportunities it offered, and the fact that the local population was not in the immediate vicinity, which made integration all the harder.

The refugee population

Emergency planning in the past has often failed to take into account the fact that, for the best part of their lives, refugees or displaced people have been entirely independent, with their own self-sufficient tribal, social, and economic networks. Finding themselves suddenly reliant on outsiders to make decisions affecting the very basics of their lives — food, water, shelter, even security — can bring a loss of confidence. This is particularly noticeable among men, who stand to lose more in terms of social status within the community and the home. *'UNHCR is now my husband and provider'* was a common cry among refugee women in Ikafe. The phrase reflected the shift away from self-reliance, and it also showed how gender-related roles had been undermined, in a way that had an inevitable impact on individual capabilities.

In the Ikafe settlement, the overpowering sense of having had every familiar reference point absolutely destroyed was often manifest in feelings of apathy. This was very evident early on in Ikafe, when the programme was primarily in an emergency phase, and people nearly always waited for Oxfam to take the lead. Representative bodies were slow to take responsibility for organisation or activities at the local level; income-generation groups lacked direction, even though self-initiated co-operatives have historically flourished in south Sudan.

In its concept of 'Ikafe', Oxfam always hoped to provide assistance in a way which would help refugees to regain their sense of self-worth, so that they could begin to take more responsibility for their own lives. The emphasis was on restoring the various capacities of individuals and communities by helping disorientated people to help themselves. This idea also lay behind the aim of 'doing relief in a developmental way'. But it did not always prove easy to use the kinds of tools and methods common to capacity-building projects, because the refugee population came from a different starting point. They were heavily traumatised, their social and economic structures had been destroyed, and many had grown accustomed to receiving handouts of relief supplies. It would be all the harder because Oxfam was simultaneously having to deliver relief services — something that in theory works against a culture of self-reliance, by increasing a sense of dependency.

'Our people have become used to receiving'

The refugees who settled in Ikafe have had a prolonged relationship with relief agencies. The war has been a factor in Sudan for the past forty years. Some people have been refugees in Uganda on and off for over thirty years; others have had access to relief aid through camps for displaced people within Sudan. Many have grown accustomed to being on the move, and have developed relatively limited mental horizons. A significant number were involved with Ugandan refugees during the 1980s — either as host communities or as employees on one of the various relief programmes. As one of the Programme Co-ordinators on the Ikafe programme explained:

> ❝ You have to remember that these refugees had not just crossed the borders. They had been in camps for the displaced in Kaya [Sudan] for two or three years, and had also seen the refugee programmes for Ugandans in the 1980s. Many could not see the difference between the donor climate in the 1980s and now. They were always making comparisons with what went on in Sudan, when agencies had a lot

more money. If they had come with no expectations, it would have been different. **❜**

The high expectations had not been diminished by one or two years in the border transit camps in Koboko, where agencies were providing a relatively high level of inputs, compared with what the Ikafe programme was working towards. A group of Sudanese staff recalled: *'In Koboko, non-food items like blankets, jerry cans and pangas were given out twice a year; and on a per capita basis. One of the agencies there cast concrete slabs for the latrines. Community health workers were already used to being paid. It contradicted everything that Oxfam was trying to do.'*

Waiting to go home

A number of the refugees in Ikafe were never really committed to the idea of settling. Those who had relatives fighting on the front lines in Sudan needed to believe that the war would be won and that refugees would soon return home. The imminent (but so far elusive) 'final push' was a constant topic of conversation among refugees. The readiness with which literally thousands of families picked up their belongings and went back to Sudan immediately after the first rebel advances of March 1997 was an indication of their lack of attachment — to any of the settlements in the region, as much as to Ikafe (although the insecurity in the region was also a significant factor).

The SPLA leaders also played their part. While wanting a safe haven for their kinsfolk, it was also in the interests of the SPLA leaders to have a population which was relatively fluid, and which would be ready to return to Sudan at a moment's notice. Their influence was increasingly felt within the settlement as the Koboko camps were disbanded. The push to return home was then accentuated during the period of insecurity. As a Dinka on his way home in August 1996 asked: *'Why wait here to die in someone else's battle? I am going back to shed my blood on my own soil.'*

In the circumstances, it is not surprising that there was little commitment to the idea of self-reliance *per se*. Many wanted merely a resting place, where they could supplement their food-aid entitlements, while they waited for the war to end.

The effects of the war years

In addition to people's expectations of relief aid, and their antipathy to the idea of settling, the long years of war had brought fundamental changes to the social and cultural structures that would be so fundamental to the reconstruction of a self-reliant society. Many Sudanese communities have more or less failed to function over the past ten or twenty years. Traditional practices have been replaced by a hierarchical and authoritarian military regime. War has brought profound changes in household composition. Consistent abuses of human rights, massacres, rape, and widespread child recruitment have all served to erode traditional values, so much so that even the spoils of war are no longer shared, and children are sometimes deserted by relatives. The prevailing culture has become in many ways one of violence rather than caring.[1]

In the refugee communities in Uganda, this cultural breakdown is complicated by the fact that people are displaced in a foreign country, and that communities are mixed up with other ethnic and clan groups, between whom there are no reciprocal ties. The following incident, which occurred recently in Imvepi, is recounted here by a member of staff to illustrate the lack of a sense of social responsibility which prevailed among many of the refugees:

> ❧ Last week, the Leader from Point C came to the compound, saying that four children were starving to death. Their mother had been referred to hospital, and the children had mismanaged the food stocks. I found the eldest, who could not have been more than 12 years old, very weak; in fact, she could not even talk. The two who follow her had gone to sell water. Imagine, walking 5 kilometres to [a Point where water is short], when they were so weak! And then there was one more little one there, very weak. I asked the Leader how they had let them get to this state. He still had food in stock, his garden was also full of cowpeas. The community could have got together and each given a little to stop them getting to that state. They are only children, after all. ❧

Moreover, the refugee communities were far from homogeneous. There were significant differences in terms of ethnicity, economic status, and political affiliation. While there was strong SPLA support within the settlement, there were also groups who had traditionally supported government troops and had fled from the liberated areas. It meant that the links essential for community-based activities would be less likely to develop of their own accord.

'I blamed God that I was so unlucky'

This lack of commitment to the concept of Ikafe was all the greater because many others had already established lives for themselves in the border camps in Koboko and did not want to move. Resettlement meant dismantling newly established social structures and economic activities, as Mary L., a single mother, explained:

> ❧ In Koboko I had built my home properly. I had my bedroom, a room for visitors, a bathroom and kitchen. I hired people to do it with

the incentive I got from teaching in the self-help school there. I really wondered how I would build it all up again. It caused me to worry. I even blamed God that I was so unlucky. **"**

People had planted crops and vegetables; others invested in small businesses. Those from a commercial background had no interest in moving to a place where the main asset was agricultural land. Others were reluctant to move farther from the borders of Zaire and Sudan, where they had friends and relatives. Another refugee, Sam A., recalls conditions in Koboko:

> **"** We had begun to establish a stable life again after fleeing from the war. There was a lot of activity, with Sudanese helping to build roads, schools, water points, and doing voluntary work — in health or administration of the camps. Most of us were already cultivating and trading, and some had become quite well-off. ... When people heard the plan of moving refugees, they lost hope. **"**

If people did not go willingly, they would never be committed to the idea of putting down roots in Ikafe. Rumours were already abounding in Koboko of unfriendly Aringa who wanted revenge for the hardships they had suffered as refugees in Sudan; and of 'people who would poison' in Terego — despite everything that the host population was declaring in public about wanting to repay their debts for their years as refugees in Sudan. The refugee leaders, who were mostly traders, soldiers, and politicians interested in staying on in and around the town of Koboko, built on these rumours. SPLA leaders and others in positions of power did not want their spheres of influence destroyed as people were scattered and mixed up across the area of Ikafe. Some of the Sudanese church leaders were against the idea of moving, because they were well established in Koboko town. Local people also gained enormously from the presence of refugees, with expanded markets and job opportunities.

All these groups were quick to voice their opinions. As a result, many people started their days in Ikafe opposed to the idea of settling at all. Jane K. explained: *'When we heard we were to be moved , we were all shocked. We said to ourselves: "When looting happens here, we run to the church; where will we go in the bush?". But they [government authorities] came anyway with police and guns and forced us to go.'* It made the challenges of building up capacity all the greater.

Tho impact of insecurity

Despite all these factors, refugees did prove that they were prepared to settle, and the majority began to cultivate and rebuild communities in Ikafe. It was ultimately the persistent insecurity which wore them down, as Dominica K. explained at the height of the insecurity:

> ❧ People will be slow to cultivate again; their first harvest was disturbed in June/July; now again the second. We will dig if we are given a safe place. Who will dig if it is all to be looted? People are scared ... If possible we would go to Sudan, and start our lives for ourselves again there, but it is impossible, and so now we are defeated ... What to do? ❧

Even for trading, which in the transits was one of the very few sources of income, it was the same story, as Cecilia S. explained in August 1996:

> ❧ It is not that we are lazy ... it is just that people are tired. They worked so hard, and now it is all going to waste. Even trading is reduced: money has been looted and bicycles taken. People do not want to be exposed [by trading openly], because they fear they will be targeted; they are not motivated to save, because they know everything will be taken. It is the looting that will finally chase people away. The worst thing is the looting. ❧

From 1996, every time refugees were reaching a stage where they could begin to consider the needs of others, or to rebuild their own livelihoods, the insecurity came into play. The young man interviewed below in November 1996 had been quite active within his community during the 'good' days of the Ikafe settlement. Yet at the height of the insecurity, he seemed incapable of taking even the smallest decision in respect of his life, largely because of an overwhelming sense of powerlessness:

> ❧ The route to Zaire is now closed, since June. The border there is full of anti-personnel mines, so our passage through Zaire to the south-west is stopped. The borders into government-held areas in Sudan are closed since 1993. Some of us have been warned not to return to the rebel-held areas. Anyone aged between 12 and 20 years, girl or boy, is handed a gun immediately they cross to the liberated areas; then all men up to 50 years are called on to fight. It is almost the same in the government areas ... The rebels here in Uganda are saying we must return to Sudan, but where can we go, and how do they expect us to get there? ❧

Just a few hours after this interview, his community was attacked, neighbours were raped, his home was burned, and he lost most of his property. A few of those who decided to return to Sudan during that time spoke of 'choosing to die on their own soil' rather than in someone else's war. Those they left behind apparently felt that they had no choices left whatsoever.

The refugees' priorities

During the period of insecurity, Oxfam learned much about the refugee community and their priorities. While it seemed impossible, for example, that refugees could be thinking of anything beyond safeguarding their personal property and lives, some apparently longer-term issues remained important.

For example, it is very common now in Imvepi to be told that refugees stayed on in Uganda throughout all the troubles simply to educate their children. Many schools in south Sudan, especially those in rural areas, are still not operational at the time of writing. Even where they are, pupils in government-held areas are regularly abducted from classes to fight in the army, while those in the liberated areas are taken for military service with the SPLA. Higher classes in GoS schools have to be taught in Arabic, which discriminates against many of the southern Sudanese children.

Ensuring that their children continue to get an education of some sort is such a high priority for most refugees that schools continued to function throughout the insecurity. Temporary centres were established in the transits and in Yumbe without any materials whatsoever, and it was only the very

below School classes were held under trees until shelters could be constructed.

Oxfam/Jenry Matthews

45

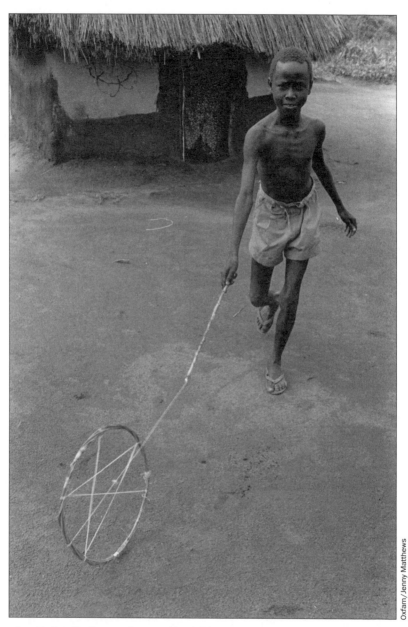

Oxfam/Jenny Matthews

above Playing with a home-made toy outside a *tukul*

young children who were kept away, by parents afraid of being separated from them in case of an attack. Children even continued to attend classes in one Point after four girls had been abducted (and two raped) from their school by WNBF rebels. Students sat through their Primary Leavers Examination with armed WNBF rebels walking up and down the aisles as they wrote. Education and further training were valued by adult refugees also: *'It is the only asset we can guarantee to take back with us'*, a Community Facilitator explained. *'It is the trainings we have had with Oxfam that may help towards rebuilding a new Sudan in the future.'*

Cultivation also remained important to refugee communities throughout the insecurity, even though there was no guarantee that crops would not be destroyed, or communities would not be displaced before harvest time. Many thousands who lost a whole crop did start to dig again for the second planting season in 1996. Others planted vegetables and cowpeas around the transit camps for the displaced. Many approached local farmers to borrow land. As food supplies were delayed, it was households with access to other sources of food or income which proved to be least vulnerable.

Many also managed to get small businesses going in the transit camps — tea shops, carpentry, bicycle or blacksmithing repairs — in order to earn some cash. Even after the first wave of insecurity, and when refugees were displaced to the transits, they struggled to retain a livelihood of some sort.

It was these factors — the sense of helplessness, the fact that livelihoods and education remained such central priorities for refugees, and that the fact refugees retained a longer-term vision of sorts — that influenced the development of more relevant programming in Imvepi.

The host population

A settlement programme implemented without any reference to the local population risks separating refugees into isolated pockets which are not sustainable. It causes resentment, and hostilities build up, especially where the host population is already in need of development assistance. For a project to be sustainable, it must also contribute to the long-term development of the host population. In Ikafe, as the consultant from the Refugee Studies Programme who visited in late 1994 advised: *'If the Sudanese are to be protected, it is essential to make every effort to ensure that the project serves as a bridge between the locals and the newcomers.'* [2]

The concept of integration is integral to social reconstruction and to sustainable livelihoods. Implicit in the idea of a self-reliant community structure is one that is *integrated* within official political, legal, and administrative systems; and within the more informal cultural systems at the local level. Similarly, central to the vision of sustainable refugee livelihoods is the need to promote household economies through cultivation or business, in the context of the natural resources, markets, and economy of the host population. If outputs are to be sustained in the future, programme activities have to be integrated into the strategies and operations of the relevant host-government departments.

Meeting the expectations of local people

In Ikafe, the experience of having been refugees themselves had shaped the expectations of the local population, something which created an extremely complex political environment. As the Project Manager put it: *'Here were a community who already knew what they wanted'*, and they were determined to make every effort to ensure that they got it. Meeting their expectations by supporting development that would benefit the population as a whole would always constitute a major challenge for the programme.

Aringa is one of the most isolated counties in Arua District. Water supply and sanitation are very poor, worse than the average for the District, in which only 25 per cent of the population has access to safe drinking water. Many homes have no pit latrines or refuse pits. The general health status is very poor, medical staff are underpaid and unmotivated, drugs are in short supply. School enrolment is low, with an estimated 75 per cent of women and 50 per cent of men illiterate; schools lack trained teachers as well as materials, and buildings are in a poor state of repair. Other infrastructure such as roads is equally inadequate.

The Aringa hoped that the influx of refugees would turn things around, and that the programme would benefit the county as a whole. For them, the 'host population' meant the whole of Aringa County, not those confined to the immediate vicinity of the settlement. Local Aringa politicians in the county headquarters of Yumbe expected tangible gains, especially in terms of social and administrative infrastructure, and were prepared to use threats to ensure that they were put in place. The following letter from the Local Councils at sub-county level [LC1–3] illustrates the tensions involved. It was sent to UNHCR in September 1996:

> ❢ One of the most important point[s] to be borne in mind is that the elders of Aringa in collaboration with Local Councillors of the area had agreed to offer their land to UNHCR for the settlement of Sudanese Refugees in exchange for social infrastructural development and

services from which the indigenous natives would benefit.

We would therefore request your office to instruct Oxfam as the concerned implementing agency to abide by the agreements we made with UNHCR, otherwise these cases which are critically noted to be common with Oxfam shall cause a lot of misunderstanding not only among the indigenous natives and Oxfam herself, but also among us and the refugees who we shall not hesitate to ask to vacate our land when developments are continuously being abandoned in it. ,

Again in August 1996, when some of the funding for the rehabilitation of a number of primary schools was withdrawn by UNHCR, Oxfam was warned by a Secretary in the Local Council 3, in an extremely tense meeting: *'If you do not agree to build a school in Kongbe, I will personally mobilise the youth to come and attack Bidibidi next Sunday'*. Such threats were often made in the full knowledge that sympathetic rebel forces were close at hand.

Nowhere were the concerns more strongly felt than over the siting of administrative infrastructure. As a member of staff explained: *'The Aringa wanted permanent schools and boreholes close to where they were living, or in sites of their choice; they expected the refugees to do the walking.'* Yumbe town, the county headquarters, was almost totally destroyed in 1979/80 following the fall of Amin, and Ikafe represented the first opportunity to rebuild and reinstate the town as a viable administrative centre.3 Local politicians never accepted that Bidibidi, the main administrative block for the agencies involved in Ikafe, should be sited within the settlement area, some 20 km from the county headquarters.

None of this helped to foster good relations. People were already angry that they had not got the jobs they had hoped for; on top of this, there were apparently no gains in terms of roads or buildings. For some, things seemed to have got worse. There were longer queues at water points, and a perceived decline in security since the arrival of the refugees, as a report from a Review held in 1996 noted: *'[The nationals complain of] an increase in crime (involving arms), more traffic accidents, social conflict and possible SPLA movement. Crime has largely affected refugees, with both refugees and nationals being implicated as perpetrators'*. For the local population, the refugees had in many ways become more of a burden than a blessing.

The settlement site

Was integration ever viable?

A number of other factors worked against integration in Ikafe. As a group of refugee staff pointed out:

> ❝ People were settled so far from the nationals that there was no one to integrate with. It was never really clear who they were talking about when they spoke of the host community. It was mostly only animals and monkeys that were living within the settlement — were we supposed to integrate with them?! It meant that, instead of being neighbours, refugees regarded the nationals with suspicion. And once there was insecurity, they became their enemies, except for the very few who were living right within the settlement. ❞

Because they were kept so separate, there was very little spontaneous interaction. Another refugee explained:

> ❝ If people are closer together, then it is easier to involve them in tasks together. Like making bricks. Refugees and Ugandans could have done it together. Then they would have both got money, and at the same time had an opportunity to share some fun and jokes together. ❞

Socio-political factors

It was not only the fact that there were very few Ugandans within the settlement area that fostered poor relations between the two communities. There had historically been political tensions between the Aringa and some of the tribes represented by the refugee population.

Social, cultural, and political issues are rarely considered in site surveys, yet they can be crucial to successful settlement. While no one could have been expected to predict the sudden influx of Sudan-backed rebels into Aringa County just as the settlement began to flourish, there had always been problems between the tribes of the Kakwa (the majority of refugees) and their Aringa hosts — problems that extend to Ugandan Kakwa on the Ugandan side of the border in Arua District. In addition, although it would be unfair to represent it as a root cause, the fact that the Aringas are predominantly Islamic, while the refugees are largely Christian, did not help to build alliances between the two communities.

In Ikafe, there were obvious divisions right from the outset. Refugees began petitioning not to be moved as soon as they heard of plans to settle them in Aringa. Two refugees explained:

❛ Towards the end of 1994, we heard we were to be forcibly moved to
Ikafe. We were all shocked. Most of us recalled the mistreatment by
SPLA soldiers of Ugandan refugees during the liberation of southern
Sudan. At that time, a lot of Ugandan refugees were raped, looted and
killed. The Aringa were among the worst-affected tribes. We feared that
the Aringas would take revenge on us. ❜

The subsequent attacks on Ikafe were seen all too clearly by refugees as their
predictions coming true: *'In Koboko, we had been warned that people would
revenge the killings in Yei, that the bones of their relatives were not at rest ... Now we
are being forced to remember their warnings'*, complained one of the Secretaries
for Law and Order after his Point had been attacked. Had some of their
concerns been considered and a thorough historical analysis undertaken
before the site was selected, 'Ikafe' or something similar might still be
standing today.

Distance from the border

Refugees were moved from Koboko primarily because of its proximity to the
border. Yet in the end, even the southern parts of Ikafe were not 50 km from
the Sudan border. Parts of Northern Extension were extremely close — closer
in fact than Koboko — and the borders were easily and frequently crossed.
SPLA presence was often rumoured, as John B. remembers: *'Early on in 1996,
we were interfered with by southern Sudanese politicians, especially SPLA soldiers
wanting to mobilise people to fight or for others to join the movement.'*

Twice between 1995 and 1996, the governments of Sudan and Uganda
agreed to move their respective refugees at least 100 km from the border. Had
this been done, it would have meant the complete closure of almost all
Sudanese settlement camps in Uganda. (At that time there were at least seven
large programmes strung along the Sudan border.)

Nor did the proximity to the border create a good environment for
settlement. The Project Manager again:

❛ In Ikafe, there was too much to and fro movement across the border.
It meant that leaders did not really come up. In Kiryandongo, people had
a sense of being more settled, and for a longer time, and they respected
the leaders who had stayed with them. Ethnic ties did not seem to matter
so much. But in Ikafe, the community could never be sure how long a
leader would remain. Or whether they were really putting the
community above political interests across the border. ❜

None of these factors had been taken into account when the feasibility studies were carried out for the Ikafe programme. Yet they had a significant impact on the speed at which refugees settled in Ikafe.

Environmental factors

As the fourth chapter will describe, Oxfam questioned whether the gazetted area would ever have been able to sustain such a large refugee population by agriculture alone. The site surveys had not taken into account lease holdings and occupancy, or extensive wetlands and upland areas. On top of this, an estimated 10–12 per cent of the population of Ikafe were formerly cattle-keepers; although some areas had been put aside for cattle-keeping, tsetse, poor water sources, and restricted grazing limited the degree to which the land could sustain a cattle-based economy.

Economic factors

Oxfam had always accepted that agricultural activity alone would not be sufficient to sustain the refugee community, yet it was obvious from the outset that the area of Ikafe could never develop very lucrative non-agricultural employment or trading opportunities with the host community. Arua District has always been cut off from the rest of Uganda, with poor roads that had been badly affected by rebels since the late 1980s. When insecurity is at a height, traders have to choose between a very slow armed convoy, which can delay traffic for weeks, because it functions only sporadically (and is sometimes attacked); or a passenger ferry across Lake Albert with a very poor safety record. Flights are often the only really safe option.

Historically, trading was always orientated northwards to Sudan and westwards to Zaire. Borders have recently opened up because of rebel advances (at the time of writing) in both countries. The SPLA liberated large areas of Yei District bordering Arua around March 1997, just a few months after forces of the Democratic Republic of Congo had taken control of the area around Aru in what was then north-eastern Zaire. Yet at the time Ikafe was conceived, trading was minimal, because of the protracted hostilities. Ikafe was a long distance from a sizeable urban population (70 km from Arua) and therefore from local markets. Once the settlement had got going, a few Ugandan traders began to visit the camps, but trade was mostly limited to agricultural produce, primarily *simsim* (sesame), at rates not always advantageous to refugees, because of high competition to sell. Otherwise within Aringa County there were very few external sources of income.

This lack of economic opportunity seems to have been completely ignored in the site surveys for Ikafe, yet, as the Business Supervisor explained:

❝ Self-reliance could be pursued only after assessing the productive capacity of the camp, its location *vis à vis* existing infrastructure — roads networks, schools, water, markets and skilled services — and the purchasing capacity of the local community. A survey needs to identify what is available locally for purchase, such as improved seeds, fresh foods, or veterinary supplies. A lot of things are manufactured from outside — like wire mesh for keeping rabbits and ducks — and business people, even small farmers, need to be able to access them. ❞

Oxfam's response to some of these factors — social, geographical, and political — is addressed in the next few chapters.

below Food distribution in Ikafe: measuring out the beans

Oxfam/Jenny Matthews

Working towards social reconstruction 3

Oxfam saw that strong community structures in Ikafe were an essential component of a self-reliant settlement. Enhancing the capacity of refugees to manage their own community would be a step towards restoring a sense of dignity. It was important to ensure that systems for delivering relief aid worked to support rather than undermine informal and indigenous systems; and in trying to meet the needs of more vulnerable groups, Oxfam had to build up the community's own capacity to deliver.

This chapter looks at three important components of working towards self-management: *registration, representation,* and *community-based food distribution*. (There were other aspects of social reconstruction, such as the management of water committees and grinding mills, but the systems for these were not fully in place before the onset of the insecurity.) The chapter then considers ways of addressing the concerns of the most vulnerable groups — those disadvantaged by physical disabilities, or by social or political factors. The chapter documents some of what Oxfam learned, and how the programmes were subsequently adapted.

Many of the problems encountered as refugees worked with Oxfam to establish systems for community management of the settlement were compounded by the extreme urgency of the situation. Programme design needed to take account of social and cultural relations within the refugee community; but finding out about such things takes time, and time was a luxury that was never available in Ikafe. To compensate for the fact that individual sectors were under too much pressure to carry out their own detailed socio-political analysis, Oxfam invested additional resources in carrying out research work. As this chapter will show, sectoral staff were then committed to adapting their activities in the light of the researchers' findings, and this meant that a much more relevant programme grew up as a result. The Imvepi programme is now benefiting from many of these lessons.

Registration

If registration is done well, it can help to build the foundations for reconstructing the social structures that contribute to a strong civil society.

Ignoring gender-related interests in the registration process, for example, or cultural issues specific to minority groups, can undermine the capacity of individuals to cope in other areas. Refugees recovering from trauma will get back on their feet more quickly in a familiar environment; disadvantaged people become more vulnerable when they are split up from relatives who could care for them. In Ikafe, many men had two or three wives for whom they were responsible; settling them together would reduce the chances that less favoured wives would be ignored.

'If only we could be together'

The speed of transfers and the fact that Oxfam had no control over the process made it difficult for staff to address the needs of multiple households and extended families. As a member of staff commented:

> ❛ It is unlikely that refugees understood at the time the significance of the truck they were loaded on to in Koboko. Those people they travelled with were to become like their kinsmen for however long they were to remain in Ikafe. ❜

'*Some families were split up entirely*', a refugee remembers. '*Others were divided, because relatives who were sick and could not travel on that day were later taken to the other end of the settlement.*'

Once people had been allocated plots, it was impossible to arrange transfers unless there was another family willing to swap. For those forced to live separately, it was an extra psychological burden. The consultant who visited in late 1994 noted in her final report:

> ❛ The method of moving people to Ikafe has already created a very serious obstacle to the refugees' ability to reconstruct their living arrangements, and to organise patterns of co-habitation in households or neighbourhoods which are most conducive to the rebuilding of social networks. ❜

It did not help that many families registered members separately, in order to take advantage of the fact that non-food items and land were distributed on a household basis rather than a *per capita* basis. It was not unusual to find a 14-year-old girl registered all alone, when in fact she had her family and support mechanisms nearby and simply needed to be transferred. Such cases made it very difficult to assess the needs of vulnerable groups and the scale of the problem.

Staff support

Registering births, deaths, and newcomers for family reunions all takes time. As a Registration Clerk explained: *'Even the refugees will agree that a lot of people are out to beat the system. It takes time to vet a family, it needs patience and proper observation. If you are not careful, your population could grow by 10,000.'*

Staff responsible for registration may need training to make sure that they are sensitive to the needs of refugees to be settled together, or to have other dependants registered with them. Yet it is a difficult process, and community input in the task of registration in Ikafe was never very successful. The Deputy Project Manager (1995–97) recalled: *'We tried to hold meetings to ask the communities to agree on how to register births and deaths, but it was always difficult to get people to register a death, because it meant a reduction in food rations'.*

Registration staff needed particularly good skills of communication, to become familiar with the community and trusted by them, otherwise they would always be seen as playing a 'policing' role, as opposed to assisting in good management of refugee affairs. Now in Imvepi, staff are allocated to specific Points, so that a sense of trust is built up over a period of time.

Family tracing

Facilitating family tracing is extremely important, but very difficult if people were separated when they ran into refuge: they often have no idea at all in which direction their relatives ran. Sara D., a Dinka woman, is just one of many who have a story to tell:

> ❧ We were attacked by the Nuer one night. We ran just as they found us; me in my night-dress. My son, he was around 13 years, was with one of the other wives. He ran in a different direction. It pains me to remember it. I heard a while back he was in a camp in Kenya. If I could be sure, I would go to find him. He is all I have left now. ❧

Unfortunately there is no universal system yet developed for refugee records. UNHCR assists in family tracing through its field offices, and work through ICRC's international database system, but it is usually necessary to have detailed names and addresses. It is still not yet possible to transfer the system for use at individual sites.

In Ikafe, a simple database was created on MicroSoft's Excel package to record refugees' details, primarily to facilitate family reunions. It also helped Oxfam to get a better understanding of the demography of the refugee population. Full details were recorded from the UNHCR registration forms, with separate tables for each household, in a way that allowed the information about individuals within every family to be accessed with a simple command.

above April 1996: registering new arrivals in Imvepi

In this way, staff would also have information to assist in planning: it would help, for example, to know how many women of child-bearing age there were in Ikafe, in order to budget for material for menstruation; or, for instance, how many Dinka households there were who would need a different type of hoe for cultivation. Unfortunately, creating the system was not prioritised early enough, and the task was finished only a couple of months before Ikafe closed.

The question of ethnically mixed communities

Every Point in Ikafe was made up of mixed tribes, largely because refugees had settled in mixed groups in the Koboko camps, depending on how they crossed the borders: the camps in Koboko were filled systematically, not according to ethnicity. This was partly because of past experience in camps for Sudanese refugees in Kenya, where the creation of enclaves had increased ethnic tensions.

However, the disregard for tribal ties did little to help rebuild social networks. Refugees maintained links that crossed the imposed boundaries of Points. The influence of some chiefs extended right across the settlement, and over the heads of Point leaders. When insecurity struck, people were quick to regroup on ethnic lines.

The representative structures set up in Ikafe might have been more effective had communities been based on clans or tribes. Having mixed communities created barriers to restoring cultural practices (which was one of the early objectives in Ikafe) and inevitably affected the degree to which refugees responded to self-help initiatives, as two refugees, Marcelina M. and Wilson, recalling life in Sudan, explain:

> ❬ Everything was under the Chief. He had a committee which assisted him in his programmes, such as mobilisation, building of schools, opening roads, constructing permanent houses and churches and stores for food ... It is up to the Headmen to organise people for activities. For example, they all sit and agree among themselves how many kilometres of road they will be responsible for, and then go ahead and organise the village to clear it. ... The different tribes compete with each other. If the Kakwa build a church, then the Pojulu will see it and have to build a bigger one. There's competition between the tribes, and that leads to development. ❭

In Ikafe, there was no such drive. It would have taken considerable planning with both the refugees and UNHCR in advance of transfers, which was not possible for the people brought into Ikafe. Moving them Block by Block would not necessarily facilitate the revival of clan or other social networks. And there were other difficulties, as the Project Manager recalls: '*It would have been difficult to give them the opportunity to group themselves together, because they were not willing to go in the first place. The problem was a combination of people not wanting to move, and others not having been given any opportunity to join relatives.*'

Despite these problems, most of the Dinka did in fact refuse to settle in their allocated plots, and reorganised themselves into two areas at either end of the Ikafe which had not yet been settled, because they feared the cultural and political implications of being split up. They were particularly afraid that, as a minority group, they would get marginalised from community affairs within the Points and Villages. There were advantages to having the Dinka living together, as a member of staff responsible for registration explained: '*It was much easier administratively to work with the Dinka. The chiefs were already in place and respected by the whole community — compared with other places, where sometimes the Point Leaders were ignored, and people failed to turn up.*' They also tended to take better care of vulnerable groups within their community.

But there were also advantages in having mixed settlements, and many people in Ikafe did not support the idea of keeping different tribes separated. Charles S. explained why: '*We are all refugees, so we should all be considered together, and not treated differently. If they had made a settlement for each of the tribes, it would have increased tensions. Like this, at least we come together and get to know each other.*' One of the few women Point Leaders suggested:

❝ A tribe per village would be OK, but to put all one tribe in one Point would isolate them. Some tribes are too small anyway — just four or five families. If you put all the tribes together, they feel they are the best. Once they become known to each other, there is not such a big problem. Why increase the differences? ❞

There are over 100 different tribes in south Sudan. Even between those whose language base is similar (the Bari speakers), there has historically been a degree of mistrust between different groups. If these refugees are one day to return to Sudan, it will surely help them to rebuild more quickly if they have already established a foundation for inter-ethnic relations. A Programme Co-ordinator argued: *'Mixing groups up gives different tribes an opportunity to learn from each other. And donors do not like to segregate, because they may be accused of targeting and favouring one tribe above another. What is important is making sure that there are mechanisms to ensure that minorities are still heard.'*

Certainly the deep-felt prejudice and mistrust that stems from cultural and political differences between the Dinka and many other tribes of south Sudan were evident throughout the time that the Dinka remained in Ikafe. There was very little opportunity for informal interaction between the groups, and it is highly likely that the prejudices will remain (on either side) as the groups return to Sudan.

Promoting traditional culture

Recognising that the mixed communities would not help in rebuilding traditional ties, Oxfam promoted cultural expression through various activities. Materials for drums were provided in every Point — a very demanding exercise, as each tribe has different types and therefore different requirements. The Deputy Project Manager justified it in the following terms: *'The work Oxfam did to assist in cultural expression was extremely popular. Drums in particular were latterly focused on by chiefs as an important means of bringing the community together, especially when people were displaced in the transit camps.'*

Representation

One of the starting points for trying to rebuild communities in Ikafe was to put in place a system for refugee decision-making that would give refugees who already felt disempowered a sense that they had some control over events. On a practical level, such a system would provide a structure through which Oxfam could work and collect information, and refugees could communicate their problems and concerns, and negotiate solutions.

The system itself immediately raised a series of questions. Would it be better, for example, to encourage refugees to re-establish traditional forms of representation, or to build new ones which would help them to integrate into the social, political, and legal structures of the host country? What was once viable in Sudan might not be relevant to Uganda, especially after the long years of war that have changed the composition of communities.

On the other hand, displaced people need familiar institutions, especially if they are to assume ownership of whatever systems are established. Popular democracy, for example, is a concept alien to most Sudanese, as it is in many African societies. (Some academics, of course, would disagree.) As Sarah K. in Ikafe put it: *'In Sudan there was not really a representative system. The chief was the overall, who mobilised for contributions — work or material. And nowadays, in the liberated areas [under SPLA], everything there is in the form of command. All things are done through orders.'* Forcing the Ugandan system on to a people unused to taking part in an active and vocal civil society would in all likelihood meet with resistance.

'All things were arranged by the Office'

Such insights into the social and political dynamics of traditional and current Sudanese life helped to build a picture of the way in which community decisions were being influenced in Ikafe. They mostly emerged from six months of consultation at the start of programme, which laid the foundation for the representative systems. The structures eventually proposed were parallel to the Local Council (LC) systems established by the Government of Uganda. It was hoped that adopting the Ugandan model would facilitate integration between the two communities on a formal level, and eventual integration with national structures when Oxfam was no longer involved in the settlement. The structures put forward were largely familiar to Ikafe residents from the Koboko camps. Committees were formed at Block, Village, Point, Zone and Council levels, with 13 members at each level. The positions included Secretaries for Law and Order, Vulnerable People, Health and Sanitation, Agro-Forestry, Distribution, Mobilisation, and Women. Only this last post was reserved exclusively for women. All posts were voluntary, and no one could hold a position at two levels.

Refugee representative structures and corresponding GoU administration

Refugee structures	GoU structures	Oxfam
Block		
Village		
Point	LC1 (sub-Parish)	
Zonal	LC2 (Parish)	
Refugee Council	LC3 (Sub-County)	
	LC4 (County)	
	LC5 (District)	Management

Some research carried out at the time outlined the characteristics of the Block committee leaders and women representatives who were elected. Almost all the leaders were young men, and over 20 per cent were students. Oxfam assumed that, as the settlement became more stable and after the initial negotiations, these would be replaced by older, more mature leaders. Most of the Women's Secretary positions were filled by younger women, many of whom were business people.

It is extremely unusual for an agency in an emergency situation to invest the sort of time that Oxfam staff put in to consulting the communities in Ikafe. Yet despite the months of consultation, the refugees in Ikafe never took ownership of the committees, and most structures collapsed as soon as refugees were displaced, to be replaced by the traditional tribal systems.

A group of refugees attending a workshop on representation in early 1997 tried to explain some other problems:

> ❟ The committees were initiated by outsiders and not the community. Many of the people elected lacked interest; they did not understand their roles, which were never clearly defined. Some people only stood as leaders because they were expecting some assistance from Oxfam. After all, it was an Oxfam structure. Not everyone elected to a post had the real capability. Then there was rivalling for leadership. ❟

Post-holders on the committees consistently complained of not having been given roles, yet were not inclined to initiate anything themselves. Particularly at the Block and Village levels, there were too many positions on the committees, leading to redundancy. People were elected through a quasi-democratic process which was not only alien to most of the refugees but was also highly flawed. There was no secret ballot; people formed lines behind candidates, which gave ample opportunity for rebel influences and other political forces to come to play. Elected representatives were mostly male and members of the educated elite, many of them politicians who were hoping for remuneration and status. They were hardly representative of the general refugee population.

One of the problems was that many of the staff who were doing the 'consulting' were inexperienced and recruited in a hurry. Their skills of communication may not have been developed enough to deal with such a complex situation, and 'consensus' may have been reported but never actually reached.

Political interests

It is very often politicians who come forward first in a new situation, because they are more vocal or are able to speak the working language in the country of asylum. In Ikafe, agencies had insufficient understanding of the dynamics of Sudanese society, especially the political influence of the SPLA. Although it was consistently denied by Ugandan authorities and by some of the Sudanese refugees, there were reports of influential SPLA/M representatives within the camp. It was alleged that some were armed; many others were simply acting as observers and informers for the Movement; some held administrative positions with the Sudanese People's Liberation Movement (SPLM), and were responsible for collecting dues, or for 'advising' refugee movement in and out of the settlement. The fact that reports of refugee actions within the settlement allegedly reached Movement officials within Sudan undoubtedly had an impact on the choices made by the refugees.

Traditional chiefs and elders

There were other people within the community who continued to hold a tacitly acknowledged power — different people for different things. Chiefs in particular remained responsible for approving and sanctioning many spheres of activity. Former civil servants, church leaders, elders, opinion leaders, and herbalists all continued to play their various roles. Yet the structure had allowed no scope for traditional leaders to assume responsibilities, in particular the chiefs.

In Sudan, the hierarchical chieftain structure remains an important institution, especially for mobilisation and maintaining law and order. Below the Paramount Chief of a District, there are Chiefs (responsible for 10–15 villages each); beneath whom are Sub-Chiefs (5–8 villages); then Headmen (each responsible for one village); then *Nyapara* or *Kurumi* (neither word translates well into English) at household level.

Although their authority has been undermined in recent years, chiefs still play an important role within the community, especially in resolving civil conflicts, providing cultural guidance, and performing rituals. They are still the first point of contact for development in an area, and for mobilising the community. They work closely with the government in maintaining law and order, and in collecting taxes. Traditional chiefs, herbalists, and opinion leaders are acknowledged by the rebel SPLA and have been incorporated into the formal leadership structures through the SPLM Revolutionary Council, which is responsible for civil administration. They also play a key role in Sudanese camps for the displaced.

Many continued to carry weight at a very local level within Ikafe settlement, yet what became known as 'the Oxfam structures' had not allowed for chiefs to assume roles of responsibility. This is not to say that chief-based structures would necessarily have been the answer. It is unlikely that they would ever have represented the community as a whole, especially minority groups, in such a heterogeneous population. Yet it was important that a form was created within any system for their voices to be heard and some authority asserted.

It did not help that in the Points the tribes were all mixed up together. 'Democratic' elections in Ikafe had effectively been imposed, along with a pre-defined structure. In Sudan, the position of chief follows family lines, with the only 'election' being at the clan level, to decide between siblings. In Ikafe, there was always the implicit understanding that elected leaders could be changed at any time; as such, they were accorded less respect. On top of this, the people voted in were those who could speak English and were therefore best able to put forward complaints. They often wielded very little overall authority, except where people with political influence had been elected.

How respect is shown

Some refugees suggested that Oxfam had not paid enough attention to the ways in which respect is won and authority asserted within Sudanese society. A woman refugee explained:

> ❮ Very few people respect the leaders in Ikafe. They have no influence with the community, because everyone is treated equally. People see them going by foot when they are called for meetings. They think: "If the office can't recognise their roles, and does not trust them, then why should we?" ❯

Voluntary positions do command respect in Sudan, and as such are sought after. As a group of the refugee staff explained:

❬ A person would not usually turn down the opportunity to do voluntary work in Sudan. But the voluntary posts in Ikafe never earned the respect from the community. People expect chiefs and leaders to get some priority treatment. If they had been given something like a loan fund, or the opportunity to purchase a bicycle, then the community might have respected them more. It is a cultural thing. If Oxfam had shown them more respect, then the community would have followed. ❭

Yet Oxfam had always been very conscious in Ikafe of the importance of not undermining any voluntary support that came up spontaneously from within the community. And in the context of an emergency, it was extremely difficult to carry out this sort of research anyway.

The top body, the Refugee Council, which represented the whole settlement, felt that it had never been formally initiated by the Government of Uganda or by Oxfam. Although this was a misrepresentation, because Oxfam management had held monthly meetings with the Council, and joint meetings with local leaders (for monitoring and planning) since early 1996, there had been no formal initiation, which the Council felt was necessary. It was not enough that Oxfam had assisted in the election process. Membership had simply been accepted and meetings begun on an *ad hoc* basis, something not common in Ugandan and Sudanese cultures, which tend towards more formal processes. The apparent lack of respect shown to the Council was mirrored at the Point level, where structures had not been formally integrated with the Local Councils.

As a result, informal systems for representation and organisation at the community level soon established themselves. These paralleled those of Oxfam, which caused problems at points where responsibilities overlapped.

'Women assume that the meetings are only for the men'
As refugees, women often find themselves by default in new positions of authority, with responsibilities in the home and community that were formerly assumed by men. At the same time, their capacity to voice concerns may have been undermined, as traditional mechanisms for expressing them have broken down.

For Oxfam in Ikafe, this begged the question of whether representative systems should support traditional communities to recreate familiar institutions, in which women have little voice in political and administrative affairs; or whether it should seek to build on the opportunity created by the refugee situation to redress imbalances in culturally imposed roles.

With only one position specifically reserved for a woman, the majority of other posts in Ikafe were given by default to men, even on service committees for grinding mills and water points, areas which are almost entirely the domain of women. Various reasons were put forward for this, as shown by the following extracts from a series of group discussions held in 1996: '*We were not brought up in the Sudan to talk when men are around; we are afraid that we would not be able to defend ourselves.*' ... '*Islam still has a big influence on us women. Culturally we have been excluded for over a generation.*' ... '*Women hear about meetings, but they do not come. They assume that the meetings are only for the men.*'

For some, there were social costs to be considered: '*My husband would not allow me to participate in public meetings. By not letting his wife attend meetings, a man claims that what a woman has is all his.*' ... '*We women do not always trust each other. They suspect that a woman who always joins the company of men will fall in love with their husbands. They also say that a woman cannot be a leader, because she cannot command respect.*' ... '*I do not go, because I spend all day waiting for water or lining up at the grinding mill.*'

Other women spoke of their lack of education. They thought that only English speakers could stand; others said that they felt shy. Some said their interests were better represented through their own separate associations.

Without a doubt, pressure of time was another factor inhibiting women from attending meetings. In the early stages, some women were spending between 10 and 13 hours a day queuing for water, often through the night. They had to cook, clean, fetch fuel-wood, manage children, and care for the sick on top of this. They were also responsible for much of the cultivation work. Men, on the other hand, reported to a researcher that they worried and rested for over 16 hours a day. Women had no leisure time, and sometimes just 4 or 5 hours' sleep a night. So men had more time on their hands, as well as the cultural mobility to attend meetings or concern themselves more with community affairs. However, many refugees suggested that having more time on their hands made them feel depresseed. Getting themselves involved in community affairs may have been a mechanism for some to deal with this.

To compensate for some of these factors, elections and meetings were scheduled at times convenient for women; emphasis was put on encouraging non-English speakers to stand, and on helping men to understand the importance of listening to women's voices. Yet one year after the first elections, women were still not well represented.

'My people thought to elect a woman leader, to wake women up'

Had Oxfam taken more of an initiative to promote women's representation, its efforts might have been successful, because many people were in fact quite open to women standing for election, as a Block leader, Margaret N., explained: *'Men do listen to women and they respect our work, if we do it well. Men do not always stop women from going to meetings. Though I am not educated, I get a chance to speak up at meetings, and the men do listen to me.'*

Moreover, women are already quite active in the 'liberated' areas of south Sudan. They were first given political rights under Anyanya's Sudan Socialist Union in 1972 (rights which were subsequently withdrawn in the 1980s). Although women have traditionally not been elected as chiefs, they have always held positions of respect as elders and opinion leaders. Now, within the 'liberated' areas under SPLA control in the Sudan, some of these women have been legitimated as chiefs within the Revolutionary structures. In fact it is only the recent governments in Khartoum which have marginalised them. A few, like Jane K., remain very vocal:

> ❩ In Kaya [a camp for displaced people in south Sudan], my people thought to elect a woman leader, to wake women up and make men to understand that a woman has her own responsibility and is a respected person. In the New Sudan, women hold big posts. They say women have rights. If a woman gives an order, and the man refuses to listen, he will be punished. ❩

Given a conducive environment, then, Sudanese women have begun to emerge as leaders. Oxfam had been reluctant to impose its own standards of gender equity, because it had wanted to restore familiar institutions which would foster better self-management; yet staff also wanted to move towards improving representation for women. The desire to respect familiar systems perhaps prevented Oxfam from looking beyond the surface of what was being presented to it. Men wanted positions of authority, in order to reclaim their social status. They may also have wanted to re-establish their domestic authority by refusing to allow their wives to stand for election. It is possible that women had simply needed the extra push which would have been given if certain positions had been reserved specifically for them.

Adapting the system

In early 1996, with help from a Kampala-based Oxfam Programme Officer, Oxfam began another series of consultations, and produced a second proposal, which accommodated both traditional leaders and gender issues.

The 'Oxfam' 13-member structure was reduced to just five posts: a Chairperson, Vice Chairperson, Secretary, Women's Representative, and someone responsible for Agro-Forestry. There was to be a committee of five at Block, Village, and Point levels. Equal representation was established on every committee: if the Chairperson was a woman, the Vice would be a man, and so on. Re-elections would be held for all service committees (shared water points and grinding mills), with men, women, the host community, and refugee populations all equally represented.

'Oxfam's' structure became just one committee out of many at the Point level, to deal with administrative issues and food distribution. Communities were encouraged to create as many other committees as they needed. Two representatives from each — a man and a woman — would then form an overall body at Point level. This would include representatives from the Parent–Teacher Association and the Health Committees, so that for the first time there was a structure for co-ordinating the bodies and activities initiated by the other implementing agencies.[1] Two members from this committee would then be put forward to form the Council, which represented the whole refugee community. There was also provision at every level for two representatives each for the Dinkas, a large 'minority' tribe, and for the disadvantaged. Efforts were made to link the Law and Order committees, which were usually headed by the traditional chiefs, more closely with the Ugandan legal system.

Words and titles with specific male connotations were changed. The term 'chief', for example, was replaced by that of 'elder', because women in South Sudan have always been able to attain the status of elder, while they have very rarely been given the position of chief. Although the two have traditionally had very different roles, they have had similar advisory capacities in some respects. It was not so easy to adapt other titles: 'agro-forester', for example, is a technical term which cannot be translated into Sudanese language and as such may be difficult for people without a good command of English to comprehend.

What happened to these structures during the insecurity?

Just as these changes were being initiated in the middle of 1996, the settlement was thrown into a state of uncertainty by rebel activities. It was still the old 'Oxfam' systems that were being used, and the resulting displacement accentuated some of the weaknesses in the system. As Points split up, most people moved to be close to their traditional leaders or kinspeople. The Refugee Council broke down entirely. It had always lacked leadership, and its position became weaker as the situation became more tense. In a workshop entitled *Working through the Insecurity,* held in February 1997, a group of refugees explained:

> ❝ Former camp leaders have lost influence, like the Secretaries for Education, Income Generation, Health, and Women. People now put more emphasis on leaders from the church, the chiefs and opinion leaders. They have always solved the problems brought to them. Before in Ikafe they were not considered to have the qualities for administration. But, once Oxfam left, people turned to them. ❞

The Oxfam structures did, however, prove to be an important reference point for administering the re-organisation and re-registration of the displaced for food and other distributions. Refugees were extremely mobile, and staff were always reacting to a changing situation. The administrative implications of the displacement were enormous, and the original Point structures were the only means of record-keeping at a time when staff could not be on the ground to carry out a comprehensive re-verification exercise. Meeting the refugees' needs was extremely difficult, because it was impossible to do assessments. As a result, Oxfam relied on figures and officers from the original Points, to try to ensure that nobody was missed out. Had staff relied only on chiefs or church people at this time, it would have been impossible to ensure that certain groups had not been neglected. Some tribes may not have had chiefs or elders present to represent them. Point Leaders at least had a list of original inhabitants from their communities, and were easily identified by displaced refugees needing to get themselves verified.

The social and economic pressures in the wake of the violence brought marked changes in gender-related roles, which had an impact on people's participation in various activities at the community level. Some men who had assumed positions of responsibility early on had returned to Sudan to look for food, to fight, or to try cultivating on their homeland. Meanwhile, some of the leaders who remained seemed to lose confidence, with a growing sense of powerlessness. It was men who had traditionally made decisions and guided communities; yet, in the face of such uncertainty, many lost confidence to speak up. Some women in particular suggested that men were more apathetic within the community, and noted how they shied away from responsibilities they had fulfilled earlier. Sometimes women came forward to fill the gaps.

Food-distribution mechanisms

Why a community-based distribution?

The method of distributing food aid can influence social reconstruction. Handing food out directly to men and women at the household level, for example, may increase their sense of dependence on external agents, and undermine established systems of organisation. WFP has been trying since the Fourth UN Conference for Women in Beijing in 1995 to ensure that food is given directly to women beneficiaries, the rationale being that, since they are responsible for the management of household resources, giving food directly to them may increase their control over it; and also that they are less likely than men to sell part of the familys's rations.

Giving food to women usually implies that food will be distributed by the implementing agency itself, rather than by the community. In Ikafe, however, Oxfam believed that, because refugee status meant that men had lost their economic self-sufficiency and self-respect, by-passing them in the food process could marginalise them further, thus perhaps increasing their antipathy towards communal affairs. Women tend anyway to collect food rations, because of culturally defined domestic responsibilities. Marginalising men entirely from the process can send out a contradictory message: that men should not be taking responsibility within the home, and that women's roles within the household are fixed.

Every system has to be evaluated on a case-by-case basis, because the balance of power is different in each situation. The lessons here refer to food distribution among displaced people, where various members of the community may have lost economic or social status, and the issue of by-passing men is therefore more significant. Where the social systems have not been disrupted, hierarchies are likely to remain in place and therefore will need to be recognised and accommodated.

A community-based approach to distribution, which was what was put in place in Ikafe, puts responsibility for management back into the hands of the people who are receiving it. Food was handed over to a Point Chairperson, who, with other leaders, then sub-divided it to Village committees. Distribution was carried out at the Block level, with agency staff involved only in monitoring the process. This mechanism showed the refugees that their own systems were as viable and respected as any which Oxfam might devise.[2]

'We prefer it when women do the scooping'

In the early days, about 96 per cent of the actual scooping and monitoring was done by men. After some encouragement to get more involved, women

above Food distribution: a woman refugee measures out oil.

gradually took on the scooping of beans, salt, oil, and sugar — the lighter items that need care and precision. In some distribution centres, women even scooped maize. Being responsible for the scooping earned them some respect from within the community: *'We prefer it when women do the scooping; we know it will come out fair. Women are more honest'*, a group of men explained. Women also felt more confident: *'Women understand themselves better. All the mistakes seem to come from the men.'*

But getting women involved without giving them related management responsibilities was not always a good thing. Distribution work is heavy and tiring, and increases work burdens which are already heavy. In 1997, some research carried out once things had begun to settle down in Imvepi looked at the whole food-distribution system. It showed that women, largely responsible for collecting and then managing food in the home, actually felt they had less control over it under Oxfam's distribution system as it operated at that time. Many did not trust their leaders: *'Sometimes the Community Leaders will come and pretend someone has missed. One time the Block leader came late at night and took some of my sugar ration, saying there was a shortage. But there is no way of checking. It could have just been for himself.'* Another complained: *'Sometimes Block leaders reduce the amount of scooping by a half inch for everyone in the Block. Then with the balance they take it and claim it is for buying exercise books and pens to register the names of those in the Block.'*

'There was no quarrelling this time' — streamlining the system

Even if these fears were unfounded, they were still deep-felt concerns for many women, and staff recognised that they needed to bring in some changes. Some people spoke of a system with which they were familiar from other camps, in which all the food items were lined up together, so that one household collected its full entitlement in one operation (rather than waiting for all the maize to be given, then oil, then pulses and so on, which can take all day). It saved women valuable time, and they felt they had more control of the process.

The main difference between this system and the community-based distribution used in Ikafe was the level of agency involvement. The process tended to be more directly controlled by the agency's Food Monitors, who watched over the actual distribution more closely. Most significantly for the refugees, the Monitors retained control of the unused sacks, so that at the end of the distribution they could take back food which had not been claimed or collected. In the Ikafe system, the full ration for the entire Point was handed over and signed for by the Chairperson, who then became responsible and answerable for it.

It was in some ways difficult for Oxfam to agree to streamline the system in the way that the community was suggesting, because it meant taking some responsibility back into the hands of the staff, and possibly undermining traditional or re-established hierarchies and systems. There was also the risk that it would be one step back on the road to distribution direct to households. Would the system still be community-managed? Would it discourage voluntary participation, because it would be perceived as more regimented and therefore imposed? The benefits of a community-based distribution were still very apparent: *'It is better for the community to give the food themselves, because they are familiar with themselves'*, a woman refugee explained. *'When someone is not present, then they can keep the food separate. They know their people.'* Yet it was what the majority of people, and particularly those whose voices were less often heard, seemed to be asking for, and it was agreed to give it a try. In fact, fears proved to be unfounded, and very little changed in terms of community management. Household names were still called out by refugee leaders, scooping was done by men and women refugees, and Oxfam staff were still present only in a monitoring capacity. Men and women were jointly involved in scooping, and equally represented on all food committees.

More emphasis was put on good communication. If a family know when they can expect food delivery, they are better able to plan for delays; similarly, if they know exactly how many scoops they are due, they can be sure they are getting their full entitlement. People were also more confident once scoops were standardised, after many utensils had got lost in the confusion of the past year.

The response was mostly positive. Women found the new system much quicker. They had previously been waiting at the site long hours while each food item was distributed separately. It could take five or six hours for the process to be completed, and the delay had been causing arguments at home when they arrived back late with no time to cook or fetch water. They also felt better positioned to monitor the process more closely: '*Usually the men gather round at distribution and chase us away. Then we get cheated ... [The new system] took less time and it was easy to prove where people missed or received too much'. ... 'There was no quarrelling this time. In fact no one was left short. We all got our right amount'*, two women reported after the system was first tested.

Yet there are still unresolved problems, and staff continue to monitor and adapt the system in Imvepi in order to overcome them. As a Distribution Monitor pointed out: [3]

> ❬ There is never any extra ration left over at the end of a distribution to share out as an incentive among those who have been involved, so people have lost interest in scooping or off-loading. People expect to get something for their efforts. And the community tends to complain at the end of the day when we take back what is left over. ❭

The impact of insecurity on food-distribution systems

Having a community-based system already in place for distributing food gave Oxfam the opportunity to explore ways to ensure that delivery was continued when staff presence was reduced during the insecurity. Had the system not been in place, it would have taken considerably longer to get things up and running, if indeed an alternative arrangement could have been devised, because staff mobility was so restricted.

At first WFP was reluctant to allow food distributions to go ahead with very few staff on the ground. Once it was agreed, a two-day training was carried out with Point leaders, even though most were already very aware of their entitlements, and familiar with the system.

In the event, it proved very difficult to monitor the distribution systems during the insecurity. Many of the changes outlined above were not implemented until the middle of 1997, and there were many accusations of less scrupulous leaders taking advantage of loopholes. It was hard to know which refugees were actually still present to receive food. It was also difficult

right Grinding maize meal: the traditional method was used when the queues at the grinding mills were very long.

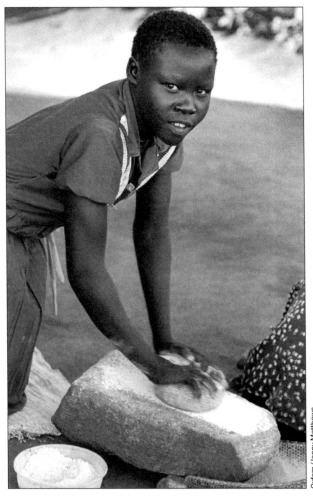

Oxfam/Jenny Matthews

for Oxfam to know how clearly messages about food delays were getting through, at a time when it was ·vital that refugees were able to plan for conserving scarce resources. As delivery delays increased, mistrust and accusations between the refugee community and local staff on the ground grew.

Despite these problems, at the time there was little else that could been have done, and the system of distribution did at least allow Oxfam to continue to provide life-saving distributions in very difficult situations. The fact that the distributions continued at all showed that some capacity for self-management had indeed been developed.

Food distribution within households

There has been some speculation that women would be more 'empowered' if they were given food directly at the household level. It was never a specific objective in the Ikafe programme to bring about changes in intra-household distribution through distributing food to women. Yet there might arguably have been some positive unintended benefits. Changes in access to and control over resources can bring shifts in power relations within the home, and access to food and cash income is often the most starkly obvious, and so more likely to induce change.

Experience in Ikafe, however, calls into question the degree to which power relations actually shift if other programme components are not present. Women do not automatically become 'empowered' just because they are bringing food into the home. In Ikafe, preferential feeding habits still discriminated against women, with men and male children eating first. In polygamous households in particular, men are expected to taste food from the stove of each wife, so they tend to eat more than their share. The only time when women in Ikafe associated food with power was when they said they were now in a position to leave their husbands, because as refugees they had access to entitlements in their own right.

Gender matters

What has gender got to do with self-management?

Becoming a refugee affects men and women in different ways — ways which are specific to their culture and situation. In Ikafe, for example, women suffered because of extreme delays in the delivery of food, poor water supply in many parts of the settlement, and a shortage of grinding mills. It all reduced the time available to get involved in community activities. Men, on the other hand, often complained of not having enough land to dig, and of there being no opportunity to earn any cash income.

Men's concerns: Underneath the complaints of the men was probably a much more deep-felt sense of having lost social and economic status. The pressures on men to provide for the home survived the process of becoming a refugee in Ikafe, while the opportunities did not, and this had an effect on both sexes. Two women explained:

❡ Here in Uganda, women make more money than men; husbands rely on women now. ... The problem is that men are poorer than women. A woman has many ways to get money. Women are also better at economising. For a man, if he got money today, he will waste it on local beer and cigarettes. Then he comes home and finds a woman still has budget, and he feels bad and beats her. Even if I had a husband, and he beat me, I'd say my husband now is UNHCR. He [sic] is now the one to provide everything. **,**

Some men could not raise the money or assets to pay dowries for the women they had settled with, and for the children whom (as it is culturally perceived) they had subsequently given him. According to cultural traditions, when dowries cannot be paid, women and children are 'returned' to the wife's parental home, and then her parents (or the woman herself) are free to look for a new partner. In other cases, women left their husbands of their own accord, to search for better prospects.

Men also suffer the effects of trauma differently, because there are fewer informal social mechanisms to help them to cope. In Ikafe it was not uncommon for them to start drinking more heavily, which in turn affected women, who suffered as male frustrations were vented in violence. The problem was made worse by the fact that the men had little to do for large parts of the day. Men and women who have lost their self-respect inevitably find it more difficult to motivate themselves, whether at the household or community level.

Women's concerns: Some women in Ikafe resorted to survival strategies which affected their longer-term positions in society. A significant number got involved in relationships with local Ugandans, including NGO staff, who had access to food and other assets. As army presence increased in the area, it was not unusual to hear of women deserting their families to stay with soldiers. A few, weighing up the short-term costs and benefits, got involved in selling sex more directly. In such cases, where women put themselves outside their own social structures, they often effectively jeopardise their longer-term security. In the future, when the market for sex declines (as the army retreats) or if the Sudanese return to their homeland, these women will be at risk of finding themselves socially and economically isolated.

A less obvious but acutely felt practical need which affected the self-respect of women in Ikafe was how to cope with menstruation. Although after the first year or so in Ikafe some families had begun to be able to purchase clothes, it was certainly not all, and very few had more than one set. Old cloth to use during menstruation was simply not available. Pastoralists have traditionally used cow-hide, but they now found themselves in Ikafe as cultivators, and cow-hide was not available. Other tribes traditionally used leaves that were not found within the settlement. Many of those who came as refugees, especially people from the urban centres, had become used to employing pads or pieces of cloth kept separately and reserved for sanitary purpose. In Ikafe, some found themselves unable to use anything. It had a big impact both on the way they felt about themselves, and on their involvement in various activities, both communal and domestic. Women avoided church services or community meetings; young girls were kept from school: '*I even missed my Primary Leavers exams*', one refugee girl reported.

Some women stopped going to fetch water or queuing at the grinding mill, because they were embarrassed to go out; others stayed away from digging, and suffered further problems as husbands complained that they were not carrying out their domestic responsibilities. As a Mundari woman explained: '*We now keep ourselves separate in our homes during that time, because of the smell*'. Some resorted to extremely unhygienic solutions, including using infants' clothes, sharing pieces of cloth with family members or friends, or picking up old pieces of rag found lying around. UNHCR soap rations were not reliable, which made it even harder for women to keep themselves clean. Women had similar problems when giving birth, in often unhygienic and cramped conditions; very often they resorted to using blankets, which were an extremely valuable asset for any household to have.

Joint concerns about reproductive health: The importance of reproductive health is often underestimated in refugee contexts, but it is a very real priority for men and women alike. The breakdown of social restraints brings new-found freedoms, especially for the young, in a society where people are living in unusually close proximity; there is a great risk of contracting sexually transmitted diseases. Some women want to deliver as soon as they settle, as a sign that things have normalised, but they have problems conceiving. Others do not want another pregnancy on top of all the other pressures of trying to set up a home. It all had an effect on how quickly people began to settle.

External constraints

At times in Ikafe, some things were simply beyond Oxfam's control. Partly this was due to the constant stress of overwork and the lack of opportunity for proper communication and consultation, and partly it was due to factors in the external environment, particularly policies of the donors, which restricted Oxfam's ability to address concerns about gender. Where blankets and plastic sheets for shelter were in short supply, distribution staff were obliged to allocate items on very poor ratios (number of items per person/household) which did not differentiate between the respective needs of men and women. At one time, for example, Oxfam had to ask refugees displaced in Yumbe to share one tarpaulin between six people, and one blanket between five, even where people were not very close relatives. Men and women were being asked to sleep together in a way that took no account of power relations and social norms, and inevitably items got sold out. Joel K., obliged to sleep in the open under some mango trees, explained: *'How could I ask my 13-year-old daughter to share with a man who is not even our tribe-mate?'*; and Helen M. complained: *'I was expected to put up with my husband's father. This is something that we can never do in our culture. Instead we cut the sheet up; each person received a sixth. But then our share was too small to make a shelter. See, it is only big enough for the two of us to sit on.'*

UNHCR has itself noted in various documents how overcrowded conditions can put unaccompanied women at special risk of sexual violence, yet with increasing global and regional demands to meet the growing needs of refugees, essential items are simply not always available in stock.[4]

Cases like this are beyond the direct control of an implementing agency, which can do little but lobby to ensure that distribution ratios do not undermine human dignity and cultural norms of decency. But UNHCR was itself already struggling to find more supplies, because buffer stocks were depleted as a result of the general drain on resources in the Great Lakes region. Targeting the very vulnerable groups is one way of approaching the problem of limited supplies, but it is extremely difficult, especially in many refugee contexts where there is no time to develop a community-based approach to identifying the most vulnerable groups.

Effects of the insecurity on men and on women

The insecurity affected men and women in a number of different ways. While women may have gained slightly more status in the home, because there tended to be more earning opportunities for them than for their husbands, the income was marginal, and in other ways women's economic and physical independence declined. Mobility was severely restricted by the risk of rape; the distance from the *tukuls* to the fields also jeopardised women's control over the sale and storage of crops, because the men were more mobile and thus able to reach the fields to harvest, which enabled them to sell output at their own discretion: it was no longer a 'household' decision.

Some men, on the other hand, found themselves at home cooking and caring for children, even collecting water and firewood, and fetching local stones for grinding, because the only piece-rate work available was harvesting, which is done by women. *'Imagine: men are now doing the work of women. Is this what you call gender balance?'*, asked Alice A. at the time. Men's sense of inadequacy was doubled. Not only were they were to assume women's roles (*'Doing women's work makes them feel bad about themselves'*), but at the same time it was more visibly obvious that women were the ones providing for the home: *'He is no longer like the man in the house'*, a mother of five complained of her husband.

More women got involved in relationships outside their communities for economic benefit, and, with the increased presence of the military, there was more opportunity for selling sex. *'This condition is forcing the young and unmarried women to prostitution. They are getting used with the natives so that they can be given money or food for feeding'*, a mother explained at the time. In the prevailing atmosphere of insecurity and overcrowding, community controls broke down even further, and refugee communities found that they had very little power to force soldiers or others to conform to any traditional responsibilities to pay dowries: *'In Sudan, parents could keep control of young girls; they were often kept inside. Even before the insecurity, in Ikafe if someone played with another person's daughter, she was given to him in marriage. Now because of hunger, anyone resorts to anything'*. ... *'Parents have no power over soldiers. How can we quarrel for goats when the man is holding a gun? We are only refugees here. Which authority could we turn to?'*

Addressing gender-related issues

Although the demands of emergency planning in the early days allowed little opportunity to address gender issues, planning at later stages in most of the sectors did take account of such concerns: registration and land allocation, for example, recognised specific gender needs, like providing for polygamous households. The early representative structures had at least tried to address gender issues, but had not managed to accommodate women, because the constraints were not properly understood. Some reproductive health needs were addressed early on in Imvepi, with family planning incorporated into the outreach programme, and cloth distributed to all women of child-bearing age for menstruation. But in many cases, gender-related needs were assessed and addressed on an *ad hoc* basis.

Part of the problem was that there was never any overall strategy. There was an assumption that gender issues would automatically be addressed within each sector — and probably by the women therein. Oxfam wanted to avoid targeting only women. As the Deputy Project Manager has pointed out: *'We wanted to avoid women-specific projects, because they would not have been helpful within the broader framework of improving gender relations, especially intra-household; and particularly in a socio-political environment where gender relations had already been so disrupted.'*

However, in some respects it would have been appropriate to promote gender-fair policies more directly. On the subject of law and order within the settlement, for example, it should have been possible to ensure that internal regulations, covering divorce or separation, took account of the different needs of men and women. Men in particular, and especially those from the towns who had more difficulty adapting to refugee life, needed off-farm opportunities for generating income. Adult literacy classes and skills training could have enhanced the position of men and women both economically and psychologically; both were proposed in Ikafe in 1996, but the plans were thwarted by the insecurity. Getting people more involved in reconstructing cultural activities, and the very process of clearing, building, planting, and reconstructing their lives, can be important means of building up refugees' self-respect. Gender-based groups, focusing on income generating or communal farming activities, emerged spontaneously in Ikafe, based mostly on traditional systems of reciprocal work relationships (*limlim*). They were an important mechanism for people to get together and discuss common concerns.

Getting gender issues on the agenda

Part of the problem was not having sufficient capacity among the staff. Although staff were given some training in gender awareness, it was only a very basic introduction. Managers needed help in setting, implementing, and measuring gender-related objectives. As the Deputy Project Manager has explained: *'While it is true that a co-ordinated gender strategy was lacking, gender issues were repeatedly included in the workplans for the programme. One of the major problems was that staff did not have a good enough understanding of what "gender" actually entailed. It was once again a problem of not being able to recruit the right staff* — and of not having the space and time to upgrade their skills of analysis.

Having somebody solely responsible for gender issues might have helped in Ikafe. Significant progress was made when a Programme Officer with responsibility for gender was seconded to the project. Most staff have specialist skills and need help in broadbased areas like gender and participation. A Gender Officer could have given on-going training at different levels, and worked with managers in planning and monitoring activities with a thorough gender analysis. Having someone specifically responsible would have helped to build on opportunities and explore new areas, like adult literacy or HIV/AIDS awareness. Many of the issues were subsequently highlighted through social research, but a Gender Officer might have been better positioned to push them forward.

There is always the danger, however, that gender issues will become excluded from mainstream programming if someone is given specific responsibility for them. The emphasis should always be on enhancing the skills of individual staff to analyse and understand gender issues as an essential part of their work. But having a more comprehensive and co-ordinated strategy would have ensured that programmes were monitored from a gender perspective, and managers themselves made more accountable.

Terminology

Careful use of language in developing activities can work to enhance women's involvement. A female member of staff explained:

> ❝ If we say we want to elect "pump mechanics", the assumption is likely to be that women are not eligible, because men are the ones who are good with "machines". Yet women are the ones fetching water, and if there is a pump breakage they suffer more than men, because it is they who have to walk long distances and waste time queuing. We should be saying things like "Oxfam needs to elect five women and five men to learn how to repair and maintain the water pumps". ❞

In Ikafe, terminology for chiefs and other leadership positions with particular male connotations was also changed wherever possible, in order not to discourage women from applying.

Vulnerability

Especially during the periods of insecurity, many of these gender-related factors increased people's vulnerability. Oxfam was always concerned to ensure that the various needs of the more vulnerable were met, but it was often difficult to ascertain those needs, and to identify who in particular was particularly vulnerable. It is often assumed, for example, that female-headed households are less able to cope, but this rarely proved to be the case in Ikafe, because many had husbands or close relatives within the settlement, or had even registered under their own names. Some people who would appear disadvantaged on paper in fact had good kinship networks within Ikafe, or had retained contacts across the border.

It was important not to label groups as particularly disadvantaged, unless they really were less able to function in society. Many of the refugees had been through extremely traumatic experiences, and a good number put themselves forward as being 'vulnerable', largely because they had lost much that was familiar to them. But giving them direct assistance, without fully under-standing their needs, risked undermining their own coping mechanisms and the other support systems already in place. It would not have contributed towards building up their self-reliance. On the other hand, there were groups who, because of gender or other social or political factors, were more vulnerable, but their needs were not immediately apparent. It was important initially to spend time identifying who was really 'vulnerable'.

Who is 'vulnerable?'

The original assessment in Ikafe employed conventional indicators used by UNHCR — aiming to identify the old, those with disabilities, widows/widowers, and unaccompanied minors — without taking account of any of the social support systems around them. It was a very broad-based approach, and as a result, in Ikafe in 1995, 4,000 people were initially registered as disadvantaged — a large proportion, almost 10 per cent of the total population.

Almost two years after the programme's inception, and a year after the initial verification, the community was involved in re-identifying 'vulnerable' groups, using new criteria defined by themselves. Only those who were completely without relatives were registered as being vulnerable, along with widows and widowers who had very young dependants. The survey was followed up with house-to-house visits by refugee extension staff, to ensure that no one had been missed, or listed as 'vulnerable' — and encouraged to feel so — when they were not at all. By the middle of 1996, the figure had dropped to 2,500, mostly the chronically sick, people with disabilities, widows and widowers, and the very old. The category of 'unaccompanied minor' was dropped completely, because there were apparently no cases where children had not been taken on by relatives or other people from their tribe.

Labelling people as 'vulnerable' risks making them feel less able to help themselves, particularly in a refugee situation, where there may already be a tendency towards dependency on relief aid. In Ikafe, the term 'disadvantaged' was adopted for those who fell into the categories identified above, because it was felt that it suggested a person who was less able in one or two respects only, and that there were ways of working to bring out their other capabilities.5

The changing nature of vulnerability

Physically disadvantaged people: The insecurity and consequent large-scale displacement of people meant that community support systems for the disadvantaged, which had never been good, broke down even further, and different groups became more vulnerable. People with disabilities spoke of becoming more of a burden to families who felt unable to accommodate them, and some were even left behind by relatives who walked to Koboko or Arua for safety.

Single people: As households moved closer to relatives or people from their own tribe, men and women who were alone, especially those from the minority tribes, were sometimes left with hardly any support at all. *'Women without men are suffering the most'*, the Secretary for Disadvantaged on the Refugee Council commented at the time. *'Men move all their women, children and property to the bush. Single women get left out. Some have left properties because they could not carry them.'*

It was not only women who suffered. Any single parent with young dependants was more vulnerable than ever, particularly because he or she faced problems in finding other sources of food. They could not leave young children in the transits, in case of rapid mass displacement, but the fields where they might have performed *leja-leja* (piece work) were too far for children to reach. People from minority tribes also suffered as networks based on ethnicity became more evident. *'People from one tribe move together to look for leja-leja, and they keep each other informed of opportunities and movements'*, an Avokaya woman complained. People from minority tribes lacked emotional as well as physical support.

Victims of rape: On a practical level, women who had been raped needed immediate medical attention, which was rarely available within the settlements, because health centres had been heavily looted, and qualified staff had mostly left. Many were anyway too ashamed to go. *'I didn't go to the clinic, because of the shame. It's better to just keep quiet and try to get over it alone'*, a woman from Ikafe explained. Many had been physically injured: one young girl raped by five armed men was unable to move for weeks afterwards. Besides the physical injury and risks to their physical health, victims of rape suffered emotional trauma, and there were few support mechanisms to help them to deal with it. All the women who had been raped spoke of an enormous sense of shame; some were afraid to move out beyond the immediate environment of their homes; many were demoralised and unmotivated. They complained of more domestic quarrels, and a few were abandoned by their husbands:

> ❦ Her husband left her when he discovered she had been raped by three men; it was the shame and the fear of AIDS. She returned to Sudan rather than face the shame of living on here. ❧

Dealing with trauma

Responding to psycho-social needs is important, because the restoration of self-respect is essential in enabling men and women to cope with stress. Women who have suffered rape, men and women who have gone through prolonged trauma, and single people who find themselves without community networks may all need help in different ways, especially because friends and relatives are either not present, or may be unable (because of their own concerns) to offer support.

Providing psycho-social care is always a difficult issue. It is generally recognised that it is important to understand how people's capabilities are affected by the impact of rape, the losses of war, or displacement. Yet professional responses to psycho-social needs are highly contested. 'Counselling', for example, confers a social stigma in very many societies, and people receiving counselling expose themselves to social ostracisation. Women who have been raped are anyway keen to avoid anything that might attract attention and fuel gossip or allegations against them. Counselling may be relevant only to certain cultures: it tends to represent a European idea of what mental health comprises.

However, in Ikafe it was likely that the specific emotional needs of individual men and women would not be addressed in a situation where everybody already felt that they were suffering. The assumption was often implicit that, because everyone was affected, people should pull together and brush aside individual concerns.

In Ikafe, Oxfam was faced with the dilemma of wanting to provide some sort of psycho-social support to individuals, but at the same time not wanting to devalue cultural mechanisms, or put individuals at risk socially because of the stigma of counselling. One manager explained:

> ❢ We were painfully aware of not wanting to impose Western methodologies, and of not wanting to force things on to people, yet there may have been times when the specific needs of individuals, such as women who had been raped, went unaddressed. Some women and men may have been reluctant to open up their concerns within their communities, and talking to a stranger may have offered an important release. ❢

Building on what is at hand
Recognising that direct counselling might not be the answer, because it risked stigmatising people even further, and might not anyway have been culturally relevant, staff began to look for opportunities from within the community to support traumatised refugees.

Group activities: Traditional ways of healing were investigated, in order to identify any indigenous mechanisms that could be built upon. At a workshop held in December 1996, for example, some of the refugee Research Team reported: *'The church mostly gives religious counselling, while the elders and older relatives tell stories to relate the things now happening to times gone by. They try to offer advice.'* These groups were then approached, to try to identify areas in which Oxfam could provide support. Some of the chiefs and elders asked for drums as a way of bringing people together in a familiar activity within the camps for the displaced. Drums have traditionally been used for a range of communal activities, including religious ceremonies, hunting, and celebrations. Young people cleared football and volleyball grounds and requested sports equipment.

Although some were afraid that any activity might attract too much attention to the transits, at a time when refugee settlements were still being attacked, the fact that the community emphasised group activities, as opposed to dealing with trauma on a one-to-one basis, was significant.

Related programming: Oxfam also recognised that the process of clearing land, digging, and generally reconstructing their lives was in itself important for the refugees. The Country Representative argued from experience that *'development activities (such as building homes or farming) are the best form of rehabilitation for traumatised people, since "counselling" takes place more spontaneously as people interact with each other in a positive environment'*.

Efforts were made to continue longer-term activities in the transits. Seeds were distributed, and opportunities for disbursing loans explored, so that people could get on with their lives to some extent throughout the difficult periods. This helped in less obvious ways. We have already seen how men and women may lose or gain social and economic status as a result of becoming refugees. The Deputy Country Representative in Uganda observed: *'It is very common that when men are redundant and poor, they tend to take to drinking, which leads to violence at the domestic level.'* Women obviously become more vulnerable as a result. Making sure that there are practical opportunities such as credit for business, or seeds and tools for cultivation, can help men and women to re-affirm their status in other respects.

Raising awareness: Raising awareness in a more broad sense of some of the psychological difficulties associated with becoming a refugee, and the symptoms of psycho-social problems, such as domestic violence, can be an important starting point in helping people to understand the sorts of problems they are (perhaps unconsciously) experiencing.

Community-based support for disadvantaged groups

Most refugees in Ikafe saw themselves as vulnerable. Well-being rankings were much easier to carry out with the host population, because the refugee community was reluctant to acknowledge economic or social stratification. They tended to be slow to care for disadvantaged groups, because many felt they had not themselves yet reached a threshold where they could start to look beyond their own immediate needs. This compounded the problems discussed above of poor leadership, the collapse of traditional kinship support mechanisms, and the fragmentation of tribes and families by settlement patterns.

Community-based rehabilitation (CBR) is about giving people with disabilities a chance to function in society, rather than treating them in isolation as 'different'. An important indicator of a society's degree of self-reliance is its ability to take care of its disadvantaged groups. Yet, even after a more realistic assessment of vulnerability had been made, it was still difficult to get communities and the disadvantaged people themselves to help themselves. A group of refugees explained:

> ❝ A vulnerable in the home is seen as an asset to the family. They are a source of additional assistance. Some of these people have been refugees all their lives. As a community, they know that a budget has been allocated for a particular class of people. In the camps in Koboko, for example, disadvantaged groups were given extra blankets and even cash. People do not want to lose that opportunity. ❞

Many of those who were classified by the conventional criteria as being vulnerable were reluctant to prove that they could function within society. When disadvantaged people were targeted for loans for a small communal farming project, for example, this preference for dependence was again apparent. The Business Supervisor explained:

> ❝ When tools and seeds were given out to vulnerable groups, it turned out that their interest was much more in getting something for free. Many left the scheme when they found it was only a loan. It was especially the case with old-age people. They expected hand-outs. Loans discouraged them, and many simply gave up. ❞

This was evident during the insecurity, when there was more emphasis on direct relief aid in the camps for the displaced, and a greater number of disadvantaged people made appeals for help. Some were victims of a breakdown in community and household responsibility, but — as it turned out — not all.

While on the one hand Oxfam did not want to alienate the disadvantaged by treating them as a separate group, on the other there was still a need to ensure that immediate basic needs were not being neglected.

Food distribution was a particular problem. The earlier Oxfam system had been criticised by both WFP and UNHCR for providing more scope for mismanagement of food, from which the vulnerable would suffer disproportionately. Research showed, however, that the biggest problem for people with disabilities was the theft of food after it had been distributed. *'At times the vulnerable groups suffer, because they cannot lift their rations. Some rough elements in the community take their food after it has been distributed'*, an elder explained.

Most vulnerable people had to rely on relatives, who may have been busy collecting their own food entitlements. One way to get around this could have been to organise a separate distribution for people with disabilities and the very old, or to hand food out directly in the home. But categorising people as a special group risked negating any sense of community responsibility, as one of the refugee extension staff explained: *'No one would help them to off-load the food, or carry it to their homes. Already by giving regular assistance to the disadvantaged, it has created jealousies and separated them from the community.'*

This had already been illustrated in the early settlement of Ikafe, when, in accordance with UNHCR policy, villages had been designed so that people with disabilities, the sick, and the very old were put into Blocks close to boreholes, to minimise the distance they had to walk. This had in fact served only to create enclaves which were avoided by the more able-bodied. Vulnerable people found themselves segregated and stigmatised.

Oxfam was aware of the need to approach the problems of disadvantaged people in a sensitive manner which would build trust and understanding within the community. People needed to understand why some individuals were being given special treatment, and to be reassured that others would not lose out as a result. Oxfam, on the other hand, needed to be sure that those chosen for special treatment were considered the most appropriate people by others within the community. It was particularly important that there was a general level of agreement for the future, as the Country Representative explained: *'We were interested in using community-based approaches, so that when rations were reduced, communities could selectively maintain increased rations for vulnerable groups.'*

Is targeting necessary?

Targeting assistance risks alienating disadvantaged groups even further from the community. Yet very often shortages of funds or goods in kind make targeting necessary. In Ikafe, staff had to make difficult choices when resources were limited: who should receive loans for agricultural production, how should shelter or clothing should be distributed? Targeting aid to refugees who all feel they are equally entitled needs careful planning and a very thorough understanding of the population, which takes time to develop. In emergencies, an agency is forced to try to share out resources as best it can.

Do disadvantaged people need extra assistance? There was always the risk in Ikafe that certain groups were appealing to Oxfam purely on the basis of their disadvantage, when in fact they were no more or less vulnerable than other groups. Yet in many respects, disadvantaged people have far less on which to fall back. For example, disadvantaged refugees in Ikafe could not supplement their food rations with *leja-leja* work, which for the able-bodied was also an important source of cash to purchase clothes and other essential commodities. Many disadvantaged people gave part of their ration to neighbours or others in return for help; but in some cases they were abused by unscrupulous people and lost out. Some were forced to sell part of their ration to purchase essential commodities or pay for the grinding mill. Others were simply poor at managing their resources, and had no other source of income to fall back on when food ran out.

There are valid reasons for targeting assistance to certain groups. But, as we have seen, it undermines efforts to build individuals' capacity to manage their own affairs; and risks ostracising disadvantaged people (and discouraging community responsibility) by giving them preferential care.

Alternative strategies

Incentives: Oxfam explored a number of other ways of helping disadvantaged groups. It initially paid youth in the community directly for the construction of homes and shelters for the disadvantaged, but this created precedents. Later on, staff considered providing additional food rations for widows, widowers, and the old to enable them to employ workers on their fields, but this idea was dropped because of the insecurity and funding problems. Discussions were recently held in Imvepi with WFP to explore Food For Work options, but such assistance to disadvantaged people did not fit in with WFP priorities in Uganda at the present time.

Traditional systems: Working towards community-based rehabilitation required a recognition that traditional civic institutions and cultural claims and responsibilities had broken down. In Ikafe, staff began in 1996 to look at traditional values and approaches to caring for the disadvantaged, in order to understand how community responsibility could be fostered and attitudes influenced. It was found that the chiefs and headmen were responsible for mobilisation in Sudan, and that the disadvantaged mostly got help with constructing their houses, digging land, and making pit latrines. This was a useful starting point for bringing in a CBR approach. Before that, everything had been directed through the refugee extension staff at Point level; and these people were always perceived as Oxfam employees. This had in many ways given the community another excuse to step aside.

Addressing physical needs

Helping a person with a disability by providing physical appliances, or enabling someone with cataracts to see again can provide an important psychological boost, as well as building up self-reliance.

The outreach physiotherapy programme to identify needs for physical appliances was strengthened, once conditions were a little safer after the insecurity. It was obvious that, even if they returned to Sudan, there would be little opportunity for disabled refugees to get appliances in that country for some time. There are still a number of mines victims in Imvepi who are young and active, and need only an artificial limb, or in some cases a wheelchair, to get them mobile again. Providing aids at a time of apparent despair gave some confidence back to people who were displaced: *'Seeing people with new limbs moving again made all the community feel happier',* an elder commented.

Social research

Most of this chapter has focused on issues which became obvious once Oxfam had a better understanding of the refugee population. It took time to uncover the cultural factors which affected programming, to understand refugees' own priorities, and to identify opportunities that could be built upon. Understanding how power relations worked in Ikafe — for example, who was making decisions, the degree to which they were accountable to the community, how traditional leadership structures had operated and how these complemented those in Ikafe — as well as assessing the potential for participation in communal activities were crucial elements in establishing programmes that would build the community's capacity for self-management.

A thorough gender analysis was needed, in order to identify the respective needs of men and of women. It was important to document current forms of social organisation and traditional structures, in order to understand capabilities within the community and to identify opportunities. Staff needed to understand what vulnerability meant in the Ikafe context, to identify those who were most disadvantaged and decide whether it would be possible to target activities to meet their particular needs. It was also important to understand the host population: were there local customs which would affect the safety and legal status of refugee women? Were the refugees putting strain ·

on resources and services such as water, or opportunities for casual labour, so that local women or men were adversely affected? What did local people feel about the influx?

In Ikafe, Oxfam was committed to an 'action-research' approach, which involved the on-going collection and analysis of information to be used for programme planning as well as monitoring. It was hoped that social research could also be used to identify in a participatory way some qualitative indicators which would measure the less tangible changes in the community. The RSP consultant recommended in her 1994 report *'developing and implementing a systematic method of measuring the impact of the assistance programme from the outset ... All aspects of the project need to be evaluated in terms of how they contribute to the empowerment of the refugees themselves.'*

It was hoped that such an approach would enable Oxfam to develop a set of sensitive indicators for the withdrawal of aid. It was likely, for example, that different households would reach self-reliance at different stages. Documenting the extent of economic stratification within the community — the various levels of poverty or wealth, or the diverse coping abilities of various households — would support a case against stopping aid uniformly across the settlement.

The refugee Research Team

Initially, research was carried out by individual sectors as a means of ensuring that programming remained relevant. A series of PRA exercises was carried out in 1995, for example, which formed the basis for the representative structures established in that year. With pressures of time in almost every sector, however, it was often not possible to develop a full understanding of the power relations which were being established in the settlement — factors such as leadership, authority, and gender-linked concerns which strongly influenced the success or failure of particular activities. Two full-time social researchers were recruited in early 1996 to explore some of these broader issues, and to help in monitoring and guiding programme activities.

Initially it was difficult to identify the best ways of working. Research needed to be closely integrated into day-to-day programming, and valued as relevant by field staff. It was important that sectoral staff did not use the presence of social researchers as an excuse not to carry out their own research work. It was also important that social research was positioned within the organisation, so that it would be able to bring about change. Social researchers and policy analysts tend to have few management responsibilities; as a result, whether or not an issue is taken seriously is entirely at the discretion of the person who manages a sector.

In addition to employing professional researchers, Oxfam recognised that some of the staff needed help in developing skills of communication and analysis which were necessary to do research work. In the end, 15 of the refugee extension staff were given additional responsibilities as part of the 'Research Team'. They represented the different tribes, sexes, programme sectors (health, agro-forestry, etc.), and zones of the settlement. The professional researchers worked closely with the team for a year, helping to collect information and plan research work. The idea was that these extension staff would then lead research within their different sectors. They continued to work as extensionists, but were given additional training in PRA methodology and data analysis, and were guided to carry out specific tasks.

The researchers themselves, in addition to doing field work, helped different sectors to identify areas where information was lacking, advised on methodology, assessed staff training needs, and carried out training to promote good practice at the field level, especially to improve communications and bring in more participatory ways of working. They also helped sector staff to identify qualitative indicators for monitoring work. Although it was still the responsibility of sector staff to collect data for monitoring and to gather information specific to their programmes, the research team was responsible for looking at broader socio-political and cultural issues, like gender or leadership; for identifying indicators to evaluate longer-term impact; and for collecting material to help managers in their lobbying work.

What sorts of data?

The researchers investigated economic stratification and off-farm income opportunities in Ikafe. This included a study of opportunities for business development, understanding traditional systems for savings and credit, documenting what was already going on informally in Ikafe, and getting a clearer picture of the potential for savings schemes. They did research into local livelihood practices, hungry periods, and coping strategies among the host population, to get a clearer understanding of the potential in Ikafe for self-sufficiency. Food security among the refugees, coping mechanisms, and systems of food distribution were also studied. Some work was carried out for Oxfam's public-health team on reproductive health, women's special needs and culturally acceptable ways of addressing them, and attitudes to and practices in family planning.

Oxfam never intended to make social research the domain of the researchers and their team alone. Their function was to build capacity in different teams, and at different levels; and to carry out more broad-based research to provide advice on social development. In the Land Use Team, for example, agro-forestry extension workers were given additional training in PRA, which was then used in carrying out a participatory assessment of specific requirements for seeds and tools distribution.

The research team continued to collect information throughout the period of insecurity. It had to be carefully guided, because refugees' priorities, including those of the refugees in the Research Team, were focused continually on the immediate security situation: something Oxfam could do little about, aside from trying to lobby the responsible government departments through UNHCR. In addition to looking at changes in leadership, research was focused on coping strategies and their impacts, and on traditional and existing healing mechanisms — issues that were anyway areas of concern for the research team in their capacity as community workers, but which in the event needed to be prioritised more actively in order to ensure that data were collected.

Some final thoughts on social reconstruction

The contradictions inherent in trying to meet immediate relief needs while building longer-term capacity were ever present in Ikafe, and especially in communal activities such as maintaining water points, cutting poles to erect school shelters, or digging shared pit latrines in the transits — where the personal gains were not so tangible. The need to act fast, compounded by pressure from donors to be seen to be performing, gave little space for a more consultative and considered approach. As a result, mixed messages were always reaching the community, as a group of refugees explained:

> ❟ The [Oxfam] office plans and arranges things before consulting the real community leaders. The Point committees get the information and pass it on. But for the community it seems to be something just pre-arranged by the office. That's why they are not active in voluntary work. They just say, "If it's something coming from Oxfam, then it should be paid for". ❟

A number of staff have subsequently put forward ideas which they feel could have instilled more of a sense of community responsibility. Grinding mills and water committees, for example, could have begun making charges right from the outset: small payments that could gradually be increased to market rates. Incentives could have been built in, such as competitions for good environmental practice, or providing bicycles to Block Leaders. A Public Health Promoter, pointing out that refugees were aware that they had asylum at the discretion of the GoU, has suggested: *'We could have worked with LCs more. If it was the local authorities going to refugees and telling them to construct pit latrines, for example, it may have had more success.'*

Opportunities could have been explored for building on traditional community-based approaches, such as the work groups known as *limlim*, in which reciprocal assistance is provided on a rotating basis. Yet there was never the time to explore all the implications of such initiatives. Only now, in Imvepi, is there room to experiment more creatively, because relationships have been built up and communication improved, and Oxfam has a better understanding of the communities with whom it is working.

below Clearing land for cultivation

Oxfam/Jenny Matthews

Working towards sustainable livelihoods 4

Social reconstruction was one important aspect of working towards a sustainable settlement. Developing self-reliant livelihoods was another. Oxfam's vision for Ikafe went beyond helping refugees to develop the ability to produce sufficient food from the land; it incorporated the ability to purchase other essential commodities, to develop business or trade, and in time to pay (either directly or through tax contributions) for essential services such as health and education.

This chapter examines how programming in Ikafe worked towards the development of sustainable livelihoods. It begins by discussing environmental sustainability. The land gazetted as Ikafe had to be able to sustain natural resources and food production for the local population and the refugees. It was vital that the quality of the land was not depleted, and that local people retained access to resources, so that they could continue to use the area as they always had, for hunting, collecting fuelwood, and gathering medicinal herbs and wild foods. It was also important that the land should provide refugees and the host population with the capacity and resources to produce food for survival and to meet their other household needs. Responsible environmental practice would need a particular approach in a context where there was very little inherent incentive, especially for refugees. Sustaining food production would involve a number of political issues regarding the rights of the local population and refugees to access to land, as well as concerns about the quality of the land in question.

Self-reliant livelihoods would involve more than simply cultivation in a context like Ikafe, where local people relied to a large extent on other sources of off-farm income, and anyway farmed much larger tracts of land than were being offered to the refugees. The second part of the chapter considers how Oxfam addressed the problems of supporting broader livelihoods in a situation where opportunities were so limited. The chapter ends by focusing on the need to integrate programming into the strategies and operations of the relevant departments of the Ugandan government.[1]

Sustaining natural resources

Forestry

Refugee settlements and transit camps in particular often have disastrous impacts on the local environment, mainly as a result of rapid deforestation and poor cultivation practices. While refugees are often welcomed because the local populace recognises the gains to be made in terms of social infrastructure and employment opportunities, the negative consequences of a very large increase in population are rarely considered.

In the case of Ikafe, the population increased in the space of less than one year from some 2,000, many of whom moved in and out seasonally, to around 47,000. Unless the land in Ikafe was protected for future use, high levels of cultivation would never be sustained. A fuel-wood-consumption survey and biomass inventory carried out during 1995 had already revealed that resources would last only ten years before widespread soil erosion took hold, and water sources dried up. It was essential that wild resources, including hunting grounds and sources of fuel-wood and medicine, were maintained, along with other culturally important sites. It was also vital that the quality of the land did not deteriorate as a result of over-use, with negative impacts on food production.

Women usually have a closer relationship with the environment than men do, because they tend to have less cash at their disposal, and the environment is considered to be 'free'. Time charts showed that the workload for women in Ikafe was considerably greater than in Sudan, especially in terms of collecting water and fuel-wood. It was important that environmental activities should improve the capacity of women refugees to manage their lives.

Links with food production

A strong forestry component was necessary in order to maintain natural resources within the gazetted area of Ikafe, but it had to be carefully constructed. Like most refugees, the people in Ikafe tended to concentrate on their own short-term needs. The immediate host communities had little experience of planting trees. The physical area around Ikafe remains relatively green and well stocked, and it can be difficult to envisage future degradation. If both communities were to invest in long-term conservation work, they needed to see some tangible returns.

The need for sustainable forestry was presented to the refugees in the context of food production. Environmental concerns were also linked into Ikafe's education, health, and business programmes. Health workers at the community level, for example, promoted the nutritional value of fruit trees;

seedling production was linked to income-generating activities. In this way, the short-term benefits were made apparent to refugees.

For the local population, forestry was mostly linked to income. Wood-lots were established and seedlings produced which offered opportunities for income in the longer term. The few centralised nurseries employed equal numbers of refugees and local people, and seedlings were distributed free of charge to both communities. Staff from the government Forestry Department worked alongside refugees to supervise wood-lots, assist in demarcating protected areas, and carry out environmental education. They also benefited from training and workshops that were periodically organised by Oxfam in Ikafe.

Natural Resource Management (NRM)

What was particularly unusual about the programme in Ikafe was its focus on voluntary activity. NRM consisted mostly of conservation of existing stock by marking trees, protection of cultural sites, and sensitising communities against irresponsible use of forest areas. Tree marking involves painting trees which should not be cut for fuelwood or construction. Wetlands, greenbelts, and forest reserves were all demarcated for protection, in places where clearing would have caused rapid denudation and soil erosion.[2] The GoU's Forestry Department was asked to monitor the demarcated areas; its staff worked alongside a team of refugees with previous forestry experience who supervised the sites and created awareness within the refugee communities of the benefits of preserving forests.

The population in Ikafe showed that refugees can be responsible in their use of natural resources if the approach is right. Tree marking, for example, proved to be a successful mechanism for preserving tree coverage. It was particularly important around the heavily overcrowded transits for displaced refugees, which had represented a very real threat to the local environment, with suddenly enormous numbers of people competing for firewood and other construction materials. It meant removing an important source of income for women who had been collecting firewood for sale, and also meant that they had to risk going farther to fetch wood for cooking. But it was ultimately essential, because no one could gauge how long the transits would be in place.

Afforestation

The second aspect of the programme was afforestation and reforestation. This included tree planting and nursery management, which was again done in conjunction with the government Forestry Department. Tree-planting

above Watering seedlings in the centralised nursery

right Seedlings were distributed free via the schools in the settlement.

Oxfam/Jenny Matthews

Oxfam/Jenny Matthews

exercises were carried out in local schools and other community centres in the vicinity; and (later, following the period of insecurity) around former transit areas. Tree seedlings were purchased from local nurseries wherever possible, in order to support the local economy. This helped to compensate for the fact that the Ikafe programme risked upsetting the local market by distributing seeds free of charge to both Ugandan and Sudanese communities.

In addition to subsidising the cost of seedlings, Oxfam tried to encourage uptake by making trees highly accessible through a series of decentralised nurseries at all Points. Rather than having just one central nursery, smaller nurseries were established within each Zone. These were privately run by refugees, with Oxfam guaranteeing to purchase 80 per cent of seedlings produced (for replanting in the locality), while the remaining 20 per cent were given out to refugees and the host population. Once these seedlings had been established and cared for within the community, a second instalment of seeds was provided to the nursery free of charge.

The benefits of this approach quickly became apparent. The nurseries did well, because they were seen as an opportunity to raise income, one that was particularly popular with the youth. A young man from one nursery group reported: *'We planted four nurseries and produced 102,000 tree seedlings. They were quite easy to raise and we also knew we would definitely be able to sell. With the money we got two bicycles, which are now helping us in other activities.'*

The scope for earning cash helped to compensate for the fact that, apart from fruit, the benefits of trees are mostly long-term. Decentralised nurseries brought trees more directly to the community, and meant that there was less tendency for forestry to become something isolated from other aspects of people's lives. Refugees were much more inclined to plant trees when seedlings were so easily accessible; and the nurseries actively encouraged good tree-care, because it was linked to future input from Oxfam. Tree planting was also linked to other sectoral activities. The youth committees which were formed to clear and maintain football pitches, for example, were given help with sports equipment only after some trees had been planted around the area.

Experience in Ikafe revealed the importance of establishing ownership of wood-lots, because for the local population trees need to be linked to more long-term benefits. Committees were established on all wood-lots within Ikafe, with their own management plans, but many of the wood-lots did not survive, because ownership had not been sufficiently established, and, once Oxfam withdrew, groups did not see any immediate personal benefit in them.

Now in Imvepi, the host community has been involved right from the outset. One wood-lot, for example, is managed by the local school, another by a youth group from the immediate locality. These people are already in a position to take over their management, and have a longer-term financial interest in ensuring their success (although it must be admitted that schools are less likely to be driven by commercial motives, so their wood-lots are perhaps a more risky venture).

It was important to look at the particular context of Ikafe, in order to identify the right types of trees to plant. What wild foods do the different communities traditionally use? And which trees do refugees prioritise? Sustaining food production for both refugees and nationals is likely to require a range of trees, because of the range of uses for tree products: to combat soil erosion, to provide legumes or fuelwood, for construction, or to protect cultural sites, for example.

There is an in-built incentive to plant trees if the end-use is properly considered. Ikafe showed that, contrary to popular belief, refugees are prepared to plant trees, if the concept is 'sold' in the right way. Christopher G. and Victoria L. are just two of the many refugees who now say they benefited from the programme in Ikafe: *'We planted fruit trees which are even now bearing fruit ... I worked hard to have good food to keep my family healthy. Then I had to leave it all uneaten.' ... 'Fruits in our homesteads had a good yield. But we left them all behind in the fields.'*

People often asked for a wide variety of seedlings, especially fruit trees and trees that could form barriers or were good for livestock or fuelwood. Identifying the right types of tree helped refugees and nationals to see good environmental practice within the context of their own livelihood systems. Fruit trees such as pawpaw and passion fruit, as well as trees with medicinal benefits such as muringa and neem, were particularly popular with refugees. Phoebe P. commented: *'We like things that bear fruit quickly. Muringa trees, for example, produce pods that can be dried and used for water; and pawpaws are good for pregnant mothers.'*

Energy conservation and environmental education

The third and fourth elements of the environment programme in Ikafe were energy conservation and environmental education. The former involved developing appropriate methods of timber and fuelwood use, especially for shelter and cooking. With over 20,000 households registered in Ikafe and Imvepi, the drain on local resources for house construction and daily fuelwood consumption was potentially enormous. Extension staff demonstrated the production of mudbricks for house construction, to replace the use of wood; and promoted the use of improved cooking stoves and saucepan lids. The production of saucepan lids was linked to the skills-development aspect of the income-generation programme. It was given an extra push during the time when people were displaced in the transits and in desperate need of cash income; and when pressure on fuel-wood resources was so great. Yet, as the Deputy Programme Manager explained: *'In reality, such measures were never a priority for the refugees, especially while the wood supplies appeared to be so good. The key to the forestry programme remained good natural-resource management and tree planting in the context of food production, which were more relevant to refugees and nationals in the short term.'*

The programme also worked closely with JRS to incorporate environmental education into the school curriculum. Workshops were held with head-teachers, education supervisors, and forestry workers. Competitions involving drama, music, and debates were arranged in Ikafe schools on a number of environment-related issues.

Rights and access to land

Much of the anger voiced by elders in Ikafe concerned their loss of access to land and natural resources. Some people who had been farming by shifting cultivation claimed that they could no longer dig land they previously worked, and there was no compensation for people whose fields now had roads running through them. Elders in particular felt that little attention had been given to important issues like the protection of sacred sites and the recognition of traditional cultural claims to land.

The legal implications of gazetting had never been properly explained to the host population. Landlords had apparently given up traditional land to which they had legal entitlements, and gained very little in return. In addition, refugees' access to the land was never guaranteed. There were no established rights of tenure for the refugees themselves, which meant that the authorities had retained the right ultimately to displace them.

Local landlords had offered the land of Ikafe in the expectation that it would be handed back to them in due course, along with all the added infrastructural benefits. Few seemed to have realised that, once 'gazetting' took place, they would lose all traditional and collective rights of access. The land that formed Ikafe was customary or public land, administered by the government. Ugandan law allows the occupant or tiller of the land to apply for tenure through appropriate administrative structures. *De facto* ownership is agreed on the basis of proof of occupancy, and leaseholds are given out for between 49 and 99 years. However, such processes are more generally sought after in urban or peri-urban areas, where disputes are more common. There is little awareness of the law, and the formalities are hardly ever practised in rural places like Aringa.[3]

Oxfam had recognised as early as 1994 that some local people had leasehold claims in parts of the settlement, but could do little more than highlight the issue to the government and UNHCR. The take-over of the Ikafe land had been negotiated at District level, and issues of compensation were never clarified to the host population. When local leaders subsequently began to demand more benefits, neither UNHCR nor the Ministry of Local Government was able to discuss the problems directly.

Poor-quality topographical data meant there was little information on current land occupation, and disputes persisted right up until the closure of Ikafe. It was particularly sensitive, because surveyors had been brought in from outside the county. In a letter written as late as January 1996, the LC4 Chairman complained: *'Simple issues like land disputes that could be solved at very lowly levels are amazingly solved in Arua or Kampala or Geneva. This happens because most of both the skilled and unskilled surveyors may be people imported from elsewhere.'*

The settlement boundaries for Ikafe were particularly contentious. They mostly formed straight lines, which did not reflect social or cultural priorities. Boundary demarcation had been carried out independently by UNHCR and government, and details of the site submitted to the Ministry of Lands for eventual gazetting as a refugee settlement. Oxfam and the local population had had no official role to play. The demarcated border areas remained a source of contention, especially because two of the Points in Northern Extension fell within a neighbouring District, which fuelled historical conflicts between two of the tribes on either side of the border.

As political tensions increased, the need to clarify issues of land use and tenure became more and more obvious. Although land had been demarcated on paper and allocations agreed at higher levels, on the ground Oxfam surveyors began to work through elders and LC members to clarify boundaries and the positions of sacred sites before demarcation. Demands for 'land purification' were later taken seriously, and eleven ceremonies were carried out in four zones across the settlement, for which Oxfam provided sheep, goats, cassava, and 'arrow money' for elders.

Sustaining food production

Besides ensuring that the settlement did not damage local livelihoods and natural resources, it was important to make sure that the local resources would be able to support the intended farming practices.

Expanding production among the host communities

While some of the local population suffered through the loss of access to land which they had always cultivated seasonally, for other households in the immediate environment a programme on the scale of Ikafe offered opportunities to diversify their farms, and improve food security. The refugee population flooded the local market with cheap labour. Many refugees needed extra income in order to supplement food rations or help them to build up assets and homes, and agricultural piece-rate work *(leja-leja)* was an important source. For local farmers, it was a chance to open up more land to cultivation. It could provide the opportunity, for example, to expand into cash-cropping: Aringa farmers have traditionally grown cotton, and the District of Arua produces large quantities of tobacco. For women and men who had been relying entirely on their own labour, it was an opportunity to bring in additional hands for the more arduous tasks like weeding or harvesting. The enlarged population also offered huge potential for marketing produce; and, as markets grew up, local people did not have to travel so far to purchase commodities.

Yet in Ikafe such opportunities needed to be actively promoted. Food production among the host population around Ikafe was already poor, partly because of lack of labour, but also because of poor resources and farming practices. Over 75 per cent of the people attending supplementary feeding programmes in both Imvepi and Ikafe health centres were local Aringa or Teregans, which suggests that food security among the host population was a major problem. The success of Ikafe would depend among other things on a strong local economy.

Oxfam recognised the importance of boosting local farming, primarily as a means of ensuring food security and strengthening the local economy for refugees and the host population. Agricultural extension work was begun with the local population in 1995, with visits by refugee extension workers to people within the locality. The team worked closely with people from the government department for agriculture.

Estimating the carrying capacity of refugee land

There were constant disputes in Ikafe over the size of population that the settlement area could sustain. UNHCR and government had originally agreed that 0.4 hectares per person was sufficient for cultivation within the gazetted area, so that a family of five would get around two hectares of agricultural land, on a *per capita* basis irrespective of age. On this basis, the original proposal for the site of Ikafe had been to settle 100,000 refugees from the Koboko border camps, but the figure was later dropped to 60,000, following surveys and resource mapping.

However, at the end of 1994, Oxfam carried out its own survey and found that the area demarcated as Ikafe would only ever be able to sustain approximately 42,000 people, even on the basis of 0.4 hectares per person, which Oxfam anyway questioned because of the poor quality of the soil. It appeared that the first surveyors had based their estimates on total acreage and had never really been in a position to assess cultivable land.

Outdated data had been used for mapping wetlands and rocky areas, and no distinction had been made between arable land, hills, valleys, or areas of varying soil quality. Oxfam estimated the land available to refugees to be approximately 27,000 hectares, which was some 13,800 hectares less than the government's estimate. Even this included areas already occupied by nationals, and there were other leasehold claims that did not seem to have been considered in some parts of the settlement.

Oxfam managers in Ikafe were consistently in discussion with UNHCR and government representatives over the issue of land capacity, yet the question was never fully solved. Three years on, at the end of 1997, discussions continued over plot size for the newly settled refugees in Imvepi. Oxfam did, however, succeed in gaining a much better understanding of the economic and environmental context in which it was working, and then tried to raise awareness of the issues with the relevant players.

Oxfam carried out its own detailed surveys on the ground, involving local people as much as possible. When similar disputes later arose over the carrying capacity of Northern Extension, for example, staff were able to negotiate better terms precisely because they had carried out their own survey in advance, and had used local surveyors who had worked closely with the host population. As a result, the intended population for Northern Extension was reduced by 4,500, because of indigenous settlement which had not been included in the original surveys.

Accurate surveys and a good understanding of local livelihood practices will facilitate much better land-use planning. The resource inventory and other socio-economic and geophysical data can then become the basis for a number of different activities, such as constructing roads, drilling boreholes, siting settlements, or establishing agricultural farming systems. In Ikafe, for example, the Dinka needed certain resources to be able to graze cattle within the settlement area, and this in turn would have had a particular impact on natural resources. Through on-the-ground surveys, and discussions with local people, it was possible to identify certain areas which could be set aside for cattle grazing. In the event, however, the land was never sufficient, and it proved logistically very difficult to administer the separate registration of pastoralists.

Participatory research was carried out with the host population to get a better understanding of how local livelihood systems functioned. It revealed that most households in the sub-county practise shifting cultivation, with land left fallow for periods of 3–5 years. As a result, they farm much larger tracts of land over the medium term. On top of this, many local farmers admitted that the refugees had not been given the best-quality land.

The contradictions exposed through these surveys put Oxfam in a better position to argue for smaller populations in the settlement. Yet it was already too late: people needed to begin farming at the same time that assessments of carrying capacity were being made. In addition, the disputes came at a time when government and UNHCR were under even more pressure to increase the size of the refugee population, because there were new refugee influxes daily.

Developing refugees' cultivation practices

Agro-forestry: The Land Use Team, which incorporated surveying, agriculture, and forestry sectors, was created in order to ensure a more integrated approach that linked agricultural practice with both environmental issues and improved land-use planning. The environment was promoted as a resource base for farmers' livelihoods; plots were allocated, and greenbelts sited, for example, firmly in the context of cultivation.

As part of the forestry programme, demonstration plots were established to illustrate the benefits of inter-cropping agricultural crops with trees for soil and water conservation. Refugees were encouraged to cultivate trees for other products like fuel-wood and fruit, and timber wood for construction.

Agricultural extension: Agricultural extension faced spacial challenges in the context of a settlement programme. Participatory assessments, for example, are more difficult in a refugee context, because communities are displaced into a new situation; but such assessments are still important, in order to develop a more holistic understanding of the constraints and opportunities perceived by refugees.

The programme began with a relatively ordinary extension approach among refugees — one which emphasised little more than mobilisation to open up land. Once cultivation had become widespread, a more participatory Farming Systems Approach was adopted for the identification and selection of technical options and the transfer of certain technologies. Agro-forestry extension workers who had been given additional training in PRA carried out a participatory assessment of specific requirements for seeds and tools to match soil quality, land size, and household seed capacity. This enabled them to distribute on a selective basis in 1996, so that the Dinka, for example, were given a different and more traditional type of hoe. The previous year, Oxfam had given a blanket allocation of seeds and tools irrespective of soil type or traditional farming practices. With this sort of information, in particular a clearer picture of indigenous technical knowledge, the farmers were helped to choose their own solutions, in the context of constraints which they had identified, which included labour, inputs, and marketing.

Crop assessments: Crop assessments were always a contentious issue in Ikafe. The objective of the settlement was to develop self-reliant livelihoods, and the gradual reduction of food aid was supposed to be linked to the ability of refugees to produce their own food. This was never going to be uniform throughout the settlement, or even within communities, because people's individual capabilities varied enormously. Oxfam was always keen to ensure that the communities were closely involved in assessing crop output, so that they were committed to and understood the criteria for the eventual withdrawal of food aid. Staff also wanted to ensure that the varying needs and resources of the community were taken into account.

However, the process proved very difficult, largely because communities were afraid of losing their entitlements to relief aid. It had been planned, for example, to reduce the allocation of seeds selectively, on the basis of crop assessments made at every Point, because some soils within the settlement were more productive than others. Although the assessments were participatory, the results were not well received, and in the end reduced allocations had to be planned on a zonal (rather than a Point) basis for the third cropping season, which was more acceptable.

Refugees' initiatives: Despite the poor quality of the land, and despite the fact that many of the Ikafe refugees came from urban areas, many thousands of people *did* begin to cultivate between 1995 and 1996. People experimented and innovated. To overcome the problems of insufficient or poor-quality land, they began to dig any land that was available, especially around their homes. Many approached local farmers for land and other resources. At times, food aid was even sold on local markets in order to purchase more seeds, especially quick-growing cowpeas and vegetables.

Even refugees from urban backgrounds recognised the benefits of carrying out some sort of cultivation, although they were not aiming for self-sufficiency from the land.

The impact of the insecurity: People displaced into the very short-term situation of the transits retained a longer-term perspective with respect to food security. When food delivery was consistently delayed, the families who were able to reach fields in order to harvest were much better off than those who could not. Others were forced to resort to extreme survival strategies like selling off very valuable assets, or risking being raped or killed in order to reach their fields.[4]

Even at the height of the troubles, refugees were asking for help with cultivation. It was recognised to be an important way of reducing future vulnerability. The very process of digging and cultivating also brought a sense of stability to a very unstable environment. A good number of the displaced, for example, returned by day to the slightly safer Points during the planting season, even though their future was so uncertain. People in the temporary transits tried to plant vegetable seeds, and many approached local farmers to lend land. Quick growing varieties became a priority, as one of the Programme Co-ordinators explained: *'In the transits, it was not possible to introduce things like tools. It was asking for them to be sold. But people did organise themselves to grow vegetables for sale, or cowpeas for food, which are all quick growing. It is very important to recognise and support these initiatives.'*

Dilemmas: There were some cases when seeds for cultivation were sold on the market, most notably when delivery of food aid was delayed, because immediate food security became the concern. At such times, Oxfam had to make difficult decisions, for instance whether to distribute seeds at time of food shortages, when the risks of their being eaten were so much greater, or to withhold seeds during a vital planting season, when planting could make a significant difference to refugees' capabilities and vulnerabilities in a few months' time, especially if the food-delivery delays persisted.

Throughout the period of insecurity, refugees still demanded seeds. But a study of on-farm activities brought up a whole series of issues for Oxfam, because it was impossible to know what the future had in store. Distributing seeds and tools while insecurity was still at its height could jeopardise future funding. Many refugees had lost agricultural tools and the seeds they had kept aside for planting when they fled — but not all. Surely another uniform handout would be a step back in terms of capacity-building? Perhaps, though, it was unrealistic to retain development objectives amid all the confusion? Many hungry refugees had anyway been forced by the situation to eat seeds or sell them along with tools. Would they do the same again? There were no easy answers, but it was important to recognise that refugees put food production high on their list of priorities, because it meant that there would be more commitment to ensuring that their input and activities paid off.

A broader approach to livelihoods

This chapter has so far looked at how the Ikafe programme approached the twin problems of sustaining natural resources and sustaining food production. Yet Oxfam had always accepted that agricultural activity alone would not be enough to rebuild the refugee community. Research had shown, for example, that most Aringa households rely on the sale of livestock to meet other family expenses like health care and education. To become fully self-reliant, all the refugees, whether from urban or rural backgrounds, would need to bring in small amounts of income to supplement what they produced from the fields.

An estimated 20 per cent of the total refugee population in Ikafe had formerly been involved in trading, business, craftwork or pastoralism, and were looking to develop more than just supplementary income from off-farm initiatives. This was particularly noticable among men, who were keen to restore their perceived economic and social status. Many former traders, accountants, carpenters, and leather workers wanted tools and materials. Traders asked for credit to help to set them back on their feet. Pastoralists like the Dinka, in addition to land, wanted veterinary services, especially to cope with the tsetse fly.

Refugees in Ikafe consistently proved that they did want to build up off-farm income opportunities. They readily formed co-operatives when loans were suggested, and with very little input they managed to get small-scale businesses up and running.

'It became almost a closed economy'

As Chapter 2 has shown, opportunities for developing lucrative non-agricultural employment, trading, or other business within the area of Ikafe were limited. Aringa County provides very few external sources of income. Cotton used to be an important cash crop in the 1970s, but has hardly been revived since people returned from exile. Aringa men and women are now mostly self-employed, do unpaid domestic work, or get an income through *leja-leja* work.

Leja-leja work in nearby farms was the only opportunity for most women and men refugees. The skills base of the Sudanese for small additional earnings was mostly not relevant to the Arua context. Many women, for example, who in Sudan had run tea-shops or got a small income from the sale of handcrafts, found the market in Ikafe virtually non-existent. Brewing local beer (*waragi*) became their only really guaranteed source of income. For men, sources of income were even fewer. As the Business Supervisor explained: *'The Ikafe economy became almost a "closed economy", with people producing only what they consumed and consuming what they produced. There was little existing infrastructure — things like road networks and markets, few skilled services — and then there was also the problem of a low-income local community.'*

In the event, people took whatever possibilities presented themselves. The younger and fitter would cycle some 30 km to the Nile to fetch dried fish for sale within the settlements. Others would travel the 70 km up to Arua to purchase smaller items for petty trading. But the local market was always limited, and the tiny trading centres that arose within the settlements did not expand significantly.

Early attempts at skills development

Development of business and other non-farming activities was perhaps the least successful of all Oxfam's activities in Ikafe settlement. The programme was hampered by the staff's lack of experience, as well as the very remote location. Workshops were initially held which reinforced traditional roles, like handcrafts for women, and promoted activities without reference to local markets or raw materials. Policy was later changed to recruit skills trainers from within the community itself, venues to be found within the Points, but insecurity once again disrupted plans. A comprehensive skills-survey was carried out, but there was not the staffing capacity to take it forward.

There were again difficult issues to consider. Should Oxfam extend its input to support the sale of produce where the local market for products was poor, to encourage economic diversification? Oxfam would never be able to sustain the intermediary role of a wholesaler. The supply of raw materials necessary to develop businesses was also a problem. As the Business Supervisor explained:

> ❝ Lack of transport always creates a bottle-neck for bringing things in.
> A programme then has to consider whether to subsidise transport, or
> provide the vehicle and get traders to contribute to the cost of the petrol.
> If the location of the camp is remote, and the road network poor, an
> agency may have to think about providing transport initially. But how
> will it be maintained in the long term? ❞

Adopting a more realistic approach to sustainable livelihoods

In 1996, an extensive participatory review was carried out in Ikafe, which provided the opportunity to think strategically for the first time about where the Ikafe programme was going, and to redefine Oxfam's aims. During the process, it was recognised that achieving self-reliance went beyond agricultural activities. As a result, the development of off-farm income opportunities became more central to the Ikafe programme.

More in-depth research was carried out after the first half of the review, to assess the feasibility of the early objectives of the programme. PRA was used to increase understanding of how the household economy of the Aringa farmers operated, so that comparisons could be made with the resources being offered to refugees. Participatory research with the refugees identified other aspects of developing off-farm income, and explored in particular the indigenous knowledge base and other prospects within the camps. Research was also done on traditional systems for credit, and the feasibility of developing a programme within Ikafe.

Developing the local economy

Refugees could not live in an economic vacuum, and the resources, markets, and economy of the host population had to be maintained, and if necessary developed, if the settlement was to be sustainable. The host population was keen to develop the local economy, and saw the refugee influx as a big opportunity. They had already allocated a plot of land in Yumbe for a refugees' market.

Refugees were not permitted however, to set up businesses outside the gazetted area, so there was no opportunity to develop the market and economy in Yumbe, which was what the local politicians and more powerful groups within Aringa had wanted. However, local people in the immediate environment did benefit enormously from expanded markets within the settlement, and the trading links which were established between the two communities were vital to the spontaneous and informal integration that was so important to developing sustainable livelihoods in Ikafe.

Recognising the importance of supporting the local economy, it had always been hoped that credit and skills development would be extended to the local population. Oxfam had planned to involve the Local Councils in identifying skills from within the refugee community, and providing or linking up with local institutions for technical advice. However, initially because of pressures of time, and later on because of the insecurity, things did not move forward quite as planned, and Oxfam succeeded in developing credit opportunities in only a very limited way and only for the refugee population.

Legal restrictions

Mobility is a vital resource for refugees in a situation like Ikafe. People needed to be able to reach markets or set up businesses in nearby urban centres. Although the Ugandan government has had a generous and enlightened approach to the settlement of refugees for the past 20 years, it was a long process to get formal permissions established, which did little to encourage refugees to diversify.

The Review in 1996 had recommended that *'Oxfam should stimulate the wider movement of refugees and the process of developing businesses and markets both inside and outside the settlement area, through a system of licences and by-laws'.* It was never easy to influence government policy over-night, but there were some small steps that the programme was able to take. Oxfam Kampala has been involved in monitoring the current revisions to the Ugandan Refugee Law, in order to ensure sure that refugees' rights to movement are respected as far as possible. This office also offered to fund a consultant from the Refugee Studies Programme in Oxford to come in and advise on government policy. But changing laws takes time, and, two years on, the final draft has still not been agreed.

High-risk credit schemes

Credit activities had begun in Ikafe with an over-ambitious strategy of community-managed revolving loan funds under the auspices of Loan Committees at the Zonal level. Credit was promised and groups formed, but nothing was ever distributed except seeds, mostly because of problems in fine-tuning the details.

Women consistently asked for loans to support activities that have traditionally earned them extra income, such as making handcrafts and brewing; yet, while staff did not want to discourage innovation, they recognised that the activities were often not commercially viable in the context of Ikafe.

During the insecurity any source of income became extremely important to refugees displaced from their homes without any independent source of livelihood. Many considered it unsafe to move very far in search of *leja-leja* work, so opportunities were limited to the very local environment; during the long harvest season, jobs were mostly available only to women. Meanwhile markets that had begun to flourish within the settlement collapsed, and small businesses failed because of low demand. Many people were obliged to resort to distress sales in very under-priced local markets.

Although it was needed more than ever at this insecure time, implementation of any form of loan scheme seemed to be quite impossible. Most community systems had more or less collapsed, and people were ever on the move. A community-based credit system was therefore unrealistic, but even giving direct loans for small businesses raised questions. Surely they would simply turn out to be handouts rather than credit, with the growing likelihood that many refugees would imminently return to Sudan? There would be little motivation to repay loans when armed looting was going on all around. The prevalence of guns in the area has always been high, and local people as well as refugees were increasingly at risk of armed attack by rebels, deserters, or other disaffected local groups.

Low-risk credit opportunities

Even during the insecurity, when people were displaced to the transit areas, the local market continued to operate, and there were still people around with money. Hotels and tea shops flourished in the over-crowded transits. There were new opportunities as the market for some services expanded: things like bicycle transport, and repairs for bicycles, clothing, and small appliances. Tailoring, furniture making, and blacksmithing also flourished; people had lost cooking pots or plates, and there was a good business for welders as many households tried to patch things together and make do.

So Oxfam staff began to explore other opportunities for giving credit. There had initially been a tendency to over-emphasise familiar forms of loans, such as credit groups, or larger-scale investment, but this sort of input was not feasible in such a turbulent situation, and as a result the programme had become unstuck. It was obvious that what might have been right in a more secure situation was not necessarily suitable in Ikafe, where the risk of a mass return to Sudan, or of renewed violence within the settlement, was ever present.

Instead, Oxfam decided to emphasise small loans, paid out directly to clients, with a very quick turn-around period. Because loans were kept small, there would never be a very great loss if the people who had taken credit returned to Sudan. The Business Supervisor reported:

> ❧ It is easy to monitor, because there is only a three-month turn around. This year [1997] in Imvepi, we gave $2,500 in loans to 19 people, chosen on the basis of gender and location within the settlement. The repayment rate has been over 90 per cent — mostly through peer pressure, with other traders acting as police. There is also the expectation of larger loans if the pilot scheme comes off. It has shown us that it is possible to design a credit scheme that can work in an emergency. ❧

Linking cash opportunities to other activities

Opportunities were created during the insecurity for a few skilled tradesmen to produce certain items that were linked to other programmes, like saucepan lids for energy conservation, and scoops production for food distribution, although in reality it was a drop in the ocean.

As the more fortunate households who had managed to reach their fields sold off their harvest at very low prices, Oxfam offered to buy seeds up at better

left A bicycle-repair business

Oxfam/Jenny Matthews

market rates to distribute for next season. It was something that would never have been considered in a normal situation, because of the risk of creating a false economy through subsidies. At the time, however, it gave people some much-needed cash.

Scaling up

If the settlement was to be sustained, it was important that programme activities were not isolated from the official development policies for the area. With a programme of the size and scale of Ikafe, there was also always a danger that agencies working in the area would simply replace the role that should be played by government. As the Oxfam House Emergencies Co-ordinator has commented: *'The scale of the whole project makes it very similar to a government scheme. Many populations may not have a government administration representative closer than 60 kilometres away.'*

Developing links with government

Oxfam always tried to link up with the local institutions and ministries which would ultimately be responsible for maintaining services in Ikafe, rather than dealing only with the government body which leads on refugee issues. Most of the activities in Ikafe — road construction, forestry, agriculture, health and education services — were closely linked to district development plans. Activities for all these sectors were planned in close conjunction with the relevant departments. Sector managers regularly met with their government counterparts, who were involved in planning and monitoring activities, as well as in implementation.

Oxfam had hoped that the Ikafe programme would enhance the ability of government departments to address local needs. District and local government officers were always invited to attend any training courses and workshops, and including government officers and extension staff in training proved to be a useful way of showing Oxfam's commitment to local institutional development.

Problems sometimes arose where department priorities varied at central, district, and county levels. The MoLG in Kampala, for example, was often more concerned with national security issues, while the MoLG at District level was interested in promoting District priorities. Tensions between the two were often high, and communication poor. Oxfam sometimes got caught up in the middle.

Ensuring sustainable services

Linking up with the government development strategy was an important way of ensuring that future use and maintenance were considered when infrastructure was sited, or services provided. Having the government forest department involved in the environment programme, for example, has meant that now in the established nurseries of what was the Ikafe settlement, the Forestry Division has quickly assumed responsibility, because staff were already familiar with the programme. The health services in Imvepi have almost 70 per cent of their staff seconded from the District Medical Office, who will in time take over.

Wherever possible, Oxfam tried to involve local government representatives as well as elders and refugees in siting any permanent infrastructure (for health and education in particular), in order to ensure its future maintenance — and future use for the local community. The site for the health centre in Imvepi, for example, is 2 km outside the gazetted area, but was chosen jointly by the refugees, the host community, and local authorities. As a result, there is full commitment from the government Medical Office and from local administration to ensure that it is maintained and used in the future.

Yet it was not always possible, and nowhere were tensions more apparent than over the siting of office infrastructure. As the second chapter described,

Yumbe town, the county headquarters, was almost totally destroyed in 1979/80 following the fall of Amin, and the Ikafe programme represented the first opportunity for rebuilding it. The local administration was keen to take advantage of the opportunity to restore Yumbe as a political and administrative centre (especially in light of officials' aspirations to establish Aringa County with District status). Oxfam was keen to give more consideration to the future use (and maintenance) of infrastructure, which would contribute to the development and sustainability of the area more generally. Yumbe seemed to be the most suitable site for office and administrative buildings.

Yet central government (and UNHCR) had their own plans for the gazetted area, which were to retain it for future influxes or other government use. It was never the intention to hand over infrastructure (especially the office and other compound facilities) to the host population once the refugees had left, and they insisted that what was to become 'Bidibidi', the main programme compound, was situated within the area demarcated as Ikafe.

As a result, in Bidibidi all the investment put into infrastructure has gone to waste. A large office block, several stores, a guest house, over 100 houses, a huge workshop, and all the facilities of water and sanitation have been simply left to rot. Just a few months after Ikafe was formally closed, the local population, who have no commitment to an area in the middle of what they consider hunting land, have looted anything valuable (like iron sheets, fencing, and window frames) and left the rest to the termites. In a few years' time, there will doubtless be very little left standing. Had it been sited in Yumbe, it is much more likely that it would have been kept up and utilised by the local community.

Linking with NGOs

Oxfam had hoped to identify local partners around Ikafe to implement development programmes for the host community. It was already funding some national NGOs, such as the National Union for People with Disabilities, with whom opportunities could have been explored. Yet with the consistent constraints on time, especially in the early days, and what amounted at times to crisis management as security deteriorated, it proved very difficult to explore other alternatives.

Support for returnees

In many situations where refugees are fleeing from war, there is always the possibility of a sudden mass return home to what is likely to be an extremely underdeveloped situation — where social and physical infrastructure in particular are lacking. Agencies and donors should perhaps consider programming which will help refugees not only in their immediate need, but in their eventual return to their homelands.

In this respect, during the insecurity in Ikafe, Oxfam deliberately increased its efforts to fit mobility appliances, conscious of the fact that there would be few such opportunities for some years to come in Sudan. But there are a number of other areas that agencies could explore.

A major focus of the work of ICRC in Arua District, for example, has been the promotion of humanitarian principles in warfare. People returning to situations of strife, or drawn into war — however unwillingly — and required to fight, might be helped by the knowledge that international conventions exist for better practice in warfare.

There is also the issue of personal safety in war-torn areas, especially places like south Sudan which have been heavily mined. There have been a number of reports of people from Ikafe falling victim to anti-personnel mines since returning to Sudan. The Deputy Country Representative has suggested that Oxfam, which has extensive experience of working in mine-affected areas, could have assisted returning refugees with information about the threats they pose, and about safe responses to them.

Finally, international organisations may be in a better position to carry out advocacy work, to try to ensure that the environment to which refugees are returning is conducive to the rebuilding of their lives. For example, one of the reasons why refugees now in Imvepi say they are staying on in Uganda is to ensure a good education for their children. Were the abductions of school children in south Sudan to cease, then more people might feel more inclined to go home. Is there something that agencies could do in the refugees' country of origin to try to influence those who are the perpetrators of violence?

Policies working against settlement in Ikafe 5

The rate at which the Ikafe settlement moved towards self-reliance would be influenced by a range of social and political issues (the attitudes of the refugees and the local community to the concept of a settlement programme), environmental factors (geo-physical and climatic), economic issues (especially local opportunities to diversify livelihoods); and also by the general political situation of the area — the level of insecurity, and the nature of the emergency.

Chapter 2 identified some of the factors that had a psychological impact on the refugees' individual capacities to settle. It also highlighted the expectations and political factors at work within the host population, which would affect how well the two communities integrated in social, political, and economic terms; and it outlined some of the environmental and economic problems posed by the site of Ikafe itself. Chapters 3 and 4 focused on programming issues, and illustrated how carefully designed inputs can help to build up the capacities of refugees and the host population.

This chapter shows how decisions of government and major donors can undermine a settlement process. As Oxfam's Programme Management Assistant for East and Central Africa has pointed out, *'We know that we always need more time to plan better, build alliances, bring people on board, talk through sensitivities ... But the problem is usually that other factors prevent staff from putting lessons into practice. There is always pressure to respond, and to get involved on terms other than those we would choose.'*

This chapter considers some of these 'other factors', and the following chapter goes on to ask what an agency can do to overcome some of the constraints.

Obstacles to social reconstruction

In theory, because the refugees had been initially accommodated in transit camps in and around Koboko, it should have been possible to transfer them to the Ikafe settlement in a phased and controlled manner. In practice, the priorities of the Ugandan government were constantly shifting in response to the changing international security situation. Having at first rejected Oxfam's proposal to move the refugees well away from the border with Sudan, the government conceived the idea of Ikafe, and *'suddenly there was considerable pressure and high expectations on the international community and NGOs to respond quickly and come up with the funds'* (Oxfam Project Manager).

This had an impact on Oxfam's own capacity to plan for refugees in a constructive way: it was always difficult to know what the future had in store. It meant that UNHCR and all the implementing agencies had to gear up extremely quickly, with the result that infrastructure in Ikafe was often not in place before refugees were transferred.

The initial transfers were carried out with a different agency at either end, which meant that figures often got confused, giving rise to discrepancies over food rations in particular. The Project Manager recalls:

> ❟ UNHCR and Red Cross were at one end loading refugees, with Oxfam receiving at the other. There was no contact with UNHCR to inform us of numbers to be transferred and to which areas ... There was usually a difference between figures sent to us by Red Cross officials and actual numbers we received on the ground. We had to use our own, which were physically cross-checked, but it made it difficult agreeing with officials, especially over food rations. ❟

Because of the confused and hurried way in which transfers were effected, families were split up — a fact which significantly undermined attempts to rebuild community networks.

An estimated 10–12 per cent of the population had formerly been cattle-keepers. Not all had come with livestock, but a significant number had, and large herds roamed the Koboko camps. Yet no attempt had been made to assess their needs or numbers before transferring, or to register them separately, which made settlement planning for the Dinka and other pastoral groups almost impossible.

Logistical problems

On arrival in Ikafe, all families were entitled to a package of 'non-food items' (provided by UNHCR and distributed by Oxfam) which consisted of a hoe, a sickle, a panga, a blanket, a plastic sheet, a cooking pot, and a jerry can. For many, these were extremely valuable assets to help them to establish a home in the settlement. The items were provided to every household, regardless of the size, so that a family of two would receive the same number of items as a family of six. As a result, many families in Ikafe chose to split up in order to take advantage of non-food items. This meant that children and spouse were often registered in Points at opposite ends of the settlement, and it was a huge logistical exercise trying to ensure 'family reunions'. Had distributions been

left A new arrival in Imvepi, issued with the standard UNHCR package, including a hoe, sickle, and panga

below, left Off-loading food aid

Oxfam/Jenny Matthews

Oxfam/Jenny Matthews

done *per capita*, rather than per household, some of these problems could perhaps have been avoided.

Right from the start of the programme, non-food items such as plastic sheets or blankets were not sufficient for the number of refugees arriving in Ikafe. Plastic sheets, for example, were provided for a population of just 20,000, when the number of new arrivals registered was over 46,000 by March 1995. Almost the whole of the northern zone of Ikafe was settled without any plastic sheets whatsoever; luckily it was at the height of the dry season, so there were no serious health risks. There were no blankets for people who had been put temporarily in the transits in 1994 and 1995, and this increased tensions. If refugees had arrived during the wet season, or before the grass was long enough for cutting, then thousands would have been exposed to the elements. It all had an impact on how quickly communities resettled.

When resources were really stretched, especially with the emergency distributions in late 1996 and 1997, Oxfam was forced to allocate goods on very poor ratios, which served only to encourage sales and left refugees no better off. Amin B, who was still sleeping out in the rain after a distribution in Yumbe, explained:

> ❬ We discussed and discussed and eventually quarrelled. Finally, we sold the sheet for 8,000 [Ugandan Shillings], only because I did not have any money to pay off the other two who had been put with us. We divided the money, but it was not enough to buy another one, even of poorer quality. ❭

For UNHCR, it is extremely difficult to plan for refugee influxes, and more especially for recurrent needs, in turbulent situations like Ikafe. Refugees lost much of their property during the insecurity, mostly through looting or being forced into distress sales. Replacing essential items, such as cooking pans, pangas, blankets, and jerrycans was something that had never been planned for in Ikafe; it had been assumed that, by 1996, two years down the line, refugees would be moving towards a situation where they could afford to make such purchases themselves, through the sale of agricultural produce, or through business transactions. As a result, UNHCR did not always have sufficient non-food items in stock within Uganda. In addition, it faced constant demands on its resources elsewhere in the region.

Inter-agency co-ordination
All the agencies involved in Ikafe had signed separate tripartite agreements with UNHCR and the government of Uganda; as a result, they each reported to them independently. This made it very difficult for Oxfam to take a 'lead' role.

Efforts to build refugees' capacity for self-management at the community level were weakened, because there was no organisation with authority to ensure that services were integrated. The AAIN health extension staff, for example, were not part of the initial 'Oxfam' representative committees. Refugee field staff were paid different rates by each of the agencies, which created tensions among disgruntled refugee staff and the organisations themselves. A member of staff recalls other difficulties caused by the lack of co-ordination:

> ❬ When we would try to suggest to [the AAIN Health Co-ordinator] how best we could improve the health services on ground, like putting an ambulance in place, they took it badly, because they thought we were trying to evaluate their work. They did not understand that we were also concerned. ... Everyone was always on the defensive, instead of trying to work out the best of improving things. ❭

In December 1994, a report commissioned from a health consultant noted the need for Oxfam to take a more central co-ordinating role in Ikafe. It pointed to the lack of information and shared plans, and warned that health provision would be haphazard unless there was a lead agent in a position to ensure co-ordination of all social welfare interventions: *'The greater the number of agencies implementing health, the greater the confusion in implementation strategies. This state of affairs does not in the long run benefit the refugees and adjacent local population.'*

There was further confusion because AAIN saw itself as an organisation providing health care in disasters, and its plans for the Ikafe programme centred on the prevention of epidemics and diarrhoeal disease, with a focus on curative health. Meanwhile, Oxfam was pushing for a link between community environmental practice and the state of health, raising awareness of preventative health measures, such as good hygiene practice, as a means of reducing disease. Oxfam also wanted to link up with the Ugandan medical system more directly. Achieving an integrated approach required continuing dialogue and agreement on systems which Oxfam was not in a position to implement, because of the nature of the separate funding agreements. A Public Health Promoter explained:

> ❬ There were no distinct operational borders, and some of the work of AAIN overlapped with Oxfam's. For instance, they were doing immunisation work, which is really preventative. Both agencies set up health extension workers, whose work overlapped, and they could easily have shared. There was a danger of conflicting health messages being sent out. Now, in Imvepi, things are quite different, because Oxfam is

responsible overall for health. Sanitation and curative work have been fused together under public health. The health messages reaching the community are the same. **❜**

Reliable long-term funding was also a casualty of the lack of clear co-ordination among the responsible agencies. A firm commitment from UNHCR or other donors would have enabled Oxfam to plan more effectively in Ikafe. By mid-1995, for example, UNHCR had promised only 50 per cent (£1.6 million) of what Oxfam had requested, and Oxfam was beginning to contemplate withdrawal from the programme. A guarantee of long-term support would have allowed more space for longer-term capacity building.[1]

Obstacles to sustainable livelihoods

Shortage of funds was one of the most damaging factors in the Ikafe programme, and it became worse as the programme moved away from an emergency focus. It proved extremely difficult to attract long-term support for the needs of refugees in such an unstable context. Funds for relief work tend to be easier to obtain than funds for 'development' work in this sort of situation. Yet donors do have budgets for longer-term funding. The Ikafe programme, however, suffered because it was caught somewhere in the middle: the environment was too uncertain to attract 'development' funding, yet it was not enough of an 'emergency' programme to be attractive to donors.

Programmes like Ikafe need donors to make a commitment to fund high-risk activities with flexible funding packages. One member of staff observed that donors need to understand that '*such work cannot be neatly packaged and presented, because it is not carried out in an operational vacuum. In reality, it is messy and unpredictable, and there is no guarantee of a "return" on their investment.*'

The needs of the host population

If the Ikafe settlement was to be sustainable, it needed to contribute to the long-term development and sustainability of the host population. The refugee economy would never function in isolation from the local markets, businesses, and traders; nor in a social and political vacuum. Oxfam wanted to support the development of the host population, both as an economic necessity, and in order to foster better relations and encourage integration between refugees and their hosts. Past experience from refugee situations globally has shown that resentment and hostilities quickly build up where the host population is already in need of development assistance, and outsiders receive substantial inputs.

In Ikafe, the Aringa had recognised the opportunities offered by the refugee programme for broader social and economic development of the whole county, and they had high expectations of what the programme should bring. They wanted to see tangible economic gains which could be measured in terms of employment and social infrastructure, especially schools, health services, or improved water services — and they wanted to see gains across the whole county: those whom they perceived as the 'hosts' were not confined to the immediate area of the gazetted settlement.

Yet the level of funding which UNHCR was able to commit for host-community development in Ikafe was mostly limited to the restoration of a few schools and health centres. Funds were confined to people living within a radius of 6 kilometres. It amounted to little more than a sweetener for a very few people in the immediate vicinity, and was never likely to have any impact on the larger economic and social context of the whole county.

Tensions were fuelled by the lack of firm commitment to support local development, and by the fact that there was very little to show in terms of infrastructure. At the end of 1996, UNHCR introduced a series of infrastructure projects in Aringa and Terego counties called 'quick-impact projects', or QUIPS, which were mainly rehabilitative/repair programmes for community centres and bridges. They were mostly funded as emergency measures to keep a volatile local population at bay. As such, they were token olive branches which came too late for the Ikafe programme. Had they been brought in earlier, they would probably have gone a long way to creating better working relationships among all the different players in Ikafe.

Ultimately a programme will never be sustainable, and relations with the host population will always be difficult, without a firm commitment from donors to fund local development. Oxfam tried unsuccessfully to raise funding, but it was even harder to come by than money for the refugee aspects of the programme

WFP policies

Retrospective food delivery: Policy and practice on the provision of food can affect people's long-term vulnerability in ways that are not immediately obvious. Food shortages cause stress to women, who carry the greatest responsibility for food security in the home, and at the same time they compound men's sense of inadequacy, because they are unable to perform their expected role of provider. When food is delivered late, or runs out early because of the greater energy requirements of an active household, people are forced to sell, barter other assets, or go hungry. In Ikafe, where many households resorted to selling parts of the ration to supplement their diet with something more palatable, more nutritious, or with more calorific value, many even had to sell rations in order to purchase other essential commodities. One staff member described the repeated shortages of food supplies as *'the single most undermining factor, second to insecurity, in achievement of impact in the Ikafe programme'*.

Food deliveries were late for much of the time between 1995 and 1997. During 1996, for example, refugees lost an average of 10 days' food ration every month. In some cases, as insecurity worsened, distributions were delayed by up to 20 days. In December 1996, over 10,000 people received food rations between 36 and 40 days late. All over the settlement, debts were incurred and valuable assets depleted, as families struggled to find something to eat.

Hungry people tend to have short-term perspectives. The sale of assets, future seed stock, and certain food items reduced the capabilities of refugees in many other respects. People were obliged to go for *leja-leja* at the expense of their cultivation on their own plots. Others got into debt. Hungry children were kept from school. Women deserted their families for men who could provide better economic security; others risked rape and even death by going back to harvest in unsafe areas.[2] This had an impact on social reconstruction, as well as on the sustainability of their livelihoods.

Despite all this, WFP policy is not to deliver food aid retrospectively, thus denying refugees compensation for late delivery and the associated loss of assets. There is some basis for arguing that a reversal of this policy, had it been implemented in Ikafe, might have helped the refugees now, as they struggle to rebuild livelihoods in Imvepi with very depleted assets. On the other hand, providing food retrospectively has some potentially negative implications. Extra rations, supplied to assist refugees in repaying debts incurred during shortages, may be dumped on local markets, forcing down market prices and thus local farmers' income, with broader implications for the development of the host population.[3]

Oxfam's Deputy Country Representative, who has been involved in food distribution on a number of programmes in Uganda, has suggested that a distinction could be made between delays in food caused by logistical problems, and delays caused by insecurity. In the latter case, some provision could be made to compensate for loss. She suggests: *'There could be a cut-off date for late delivery in cases of insecurity, beyond which food could be given retrospectively. To avoid a sudden boom of food, which would encourage sales and flood local markets, the distribution could be done over a period of time.'*

Each situation needs to be judged on its merits. In some economies, retrospective food deliveries may be relevant, in which case, agencies should perhaps consider providing it. In other cases, replacement of non-food items sold locally may be more relevant; or WFP might authorise implementing organisations to procure food locally, to pre-empt sales of rations.

The problem is that most programming decisions in acute emergencies are made in haste, with limited information. These often need to be revised later on, as the situation changes and more information becomes available. Flexibility in the decision-making process then becomes the key.

Size of food rations: People in settlement programmes are likely to have different food requirements from those who are more sedentary in transit camps. WFP has committed itself in writing 4 to policies which would support refugees as they try to settle. These include providing larger rations for people who are trying to establish viable livelihoods and are therefore likely to be more active; and ensuring additional food to provide essential micro-nutrients (vitamins and minerals) to people who are in receipt of relief aid for more than two months. Yet on the ground it is often a different picture. As a WFP Representative has commented:5 '*It is very difficult to go to donors who are already stretched, and tell them we want to increase the ration from 1,900 to 2,100 KCal. We already have problems meeting the target to provide needs for basic survival — however much we as an organisation would like to provide more.*'

Grinding mills: A shortage of grinding mills can be another reason why people sell off more valuable parts of their food ration. Many women in Ikafe complained of spending days away from their fields while queuing at the mills; some sold oil and other food rations to pay for private mills. WFP is supposed to provide one mill for every 5,000 people; yet in 1996, Ikafe was still short of seven grinding mills (on the basis of a population of 55,000). Getting access to the mills themselves may be a long process, but there are other ways of supporting the refugees, like encouraging WFP to provide at least half the rations as pre-ground maize meal; or obtaining funding to subsidise local private millers until refugees are established and in a position to make their own contribution.

Restricted mobility
Uganda's 1960 Control of Alien Refugees Act (an outdated law based on British policy to control German internees during the second world war) effectively puts refugees in isolated camps, thus restricting their mobility by segregating and isolating them. Any foreigners applying for formal employment face restrictions on the issuing of work permits.

Mobility is vital for refugees wanting to establish businesses or trade. Refugees must be given some opportunity to move out of a settlement area, to trade or set up businesses. The 1951 UN Convention provides for better employment opportunities by promoting freedom of movement and access to gainful employment.[6]

Legal restrictions can undermine people's efforts to develop business and work towards self-reliance. Although the Ugandan government interprets the 1960 law extremely flexibly in respect of the refugees in Ikafe, it does not encourage refugees to develop businesses. One of Oxfam's Programme Co-ordinators has commented:

> ❝ Government policy did have an impact. In Sudan, refugees could self-settle in towns. Here, it is government policy to keep them in the settlements. It has worked against refugees showing initiative in some respects. In Sudan, Ugandans came up with shops and business; they had freedom of travel; all they needed was a letter issued by the [refugee] chairman. Here in Ikafe, it is a much longer process. It affects the mentality of the refugees. Refugee life is seen as a punishment. ❞

The importance of communications work

6

A persistent characteristic of the Ikafe programme was the lack of communication among the various people and agencies involved. Undoubtedly this problem compounded the undermining effects of the external factors discussed in the previous chapter. This chapter considers ways of working to improve communication in programmes such as Ikafe.

It begins by discussing the importance of reaching agreement among all the different players on programme objectives and respective responsibilities. It then considers other ways of bridging gaps in communication, especially between the immediate host population, the refugees, and the agencies involved in the programme. Finally it discusses some of the issues that arose in Ikafe when Oxfam became involved in direct lobbying work.

Agreeing on objectives

Lack of communication by international and national organisations in Ikafe often meant that neither refugees nor the local population were very clear about the various mandates, roles, and responsibilities of stakeholders, and this marred working relations for Oxfam. Things were made worse by the fact that the international agencies and national authorities were not always clear in their communications to elders and Local Councils about their own objectives and commitments. Poor dialogue between local leaders, refugees, and agencies intensified mistrust between all the communities at the local level. While Oxfam was at pains to explain to local people that its hands were tied by lack of funding, the host population was invariably too angered by an overwhelming sense of betrayal to listen. Lack of communication within the settlement meant that refugees were often not aware of local cultural practices, something which added to the resentment and disappointment already accumulating within the host community. Poor communication between Oxfam representatives and refugees meant that refugees were not always fully aware of their entitlements, which had an impact on the efficiency of the distribution mechanisms, for example.

One of the most fundamental problems was the fact that there was no real agreement on the programme's goals. Because of the extreme pressures of time, there was never the opportunity for proper discussion of commitments, objectives, or expectations in advance. The Project Manager recalls: *'UNHCR did most of the physical planning — but off the record, which caused problems for the agencies on the ground. If we were to implement effectively, we needed to see their planning documents.'*

This need for transparency was echoed throughout the participatory Review commissioned by Oxfam, which took place in April 1996, just before the insecurity really took hold. The Review was a long process, involving a range of people representing all the major stakeholders: the host population, refugees, UNHCR, WFP, Oxfam staff, and government officials. Through discussion groups and meetings, and using various participatory tools of analysis, the Review brought into the open the range of agendas motivating the different players.

Conflicting agendas

The Review revealed that the government had one set of reasons for going ahead with Ikafe, UNHCR another, and Oxfam a third — yet all three were signatories to the same agreement, and were supposed to be working to the same set of objectives.

UNHCR and WFP aimed to establish infrastructure which would provide safe shelter for the present refugees and provide for any future influxes. They also wanted to encourage self-sufficiency, mostly through agricultural development, and they planned for a 50 per cent cut in food rations by the end of 1996.[1]

The priority for the Government of Uganda, at central and District levels at least, was to improve security first and foremost; the presence of refugees (with alleged rebel connections) so close to the border increased tensions internationally between the governments of Uganda and Sudan. The GoU was also keen to support the local economy, especially through infrastructural development; and to boost the recently decentralised District departments of health, education, forestry, and agriculture. Like UNHCR, the GoU spoke of retaining access to a 'gazetted area' for sheltering future refugees.

Oxfam's overall aim was to provide welfare services efficiently, and to promote self-reliance for refugees, with integration into local structures.

Meanwhile, the local Ugandan population and the Sudanese refugees, neither of whom were signatories to the agreement but who were equally important 'stakeholders' in Ikafe, had their own priorities. The local Ugandans claimed to want to shelter their Sudanese 'brothers', but their primary (though at first unvoiced) objective was to secure infrastructural and economic development similar to what they had witnessed as refugees in

left Education: always
a priority for refugees

Oxfam/Jenny Matthews

Sudan. Within Aringa, there are aspirations to attain District status, and it was perceived that restoring infrastructure in the County headquarters of Yumbe would increase their chances.

The refugees had their own priorities: to find a secure place to survive the war, where they would have access to food, water, shelter, and health services, and especially education for their children. Initially, at least, they seemed to be interested in developing the ability to supplement (rather than replace) relief assistance through cultivation and business.

Clarifying definitions

Because of these different agendas, fundamental concepts like *self-sufficiency* and *host-refugee integration* were being interpreted by different people in very different ways.[2]

Integration: The concept of integration created considerable barriers. Host populations defined it in terms of economic and social development, with quantifiable gains through the provision of shared resources, especially for improvements to schools, health care, and water services. Government was keen to attract resources to develop the local economy, and to develop its departments at District level through training and other in-puts. It wanted planning to be carried out with and through relevant government departments.

The refugees wanted to integrate their administrative and particularly legal systems within the formal Ugandan structures, to ensure law and order within the settlement, for example. They also expected some degree of interaction at markets and through trading, but they were keen to maintain their own identity.

For Oxfam, integration was a mechanism to ensure the sustainability of the programme. The Annual Report for Ikafe in 1995 spoke of incorporating Ikafe into 'the socio-legal, economic and administrative structures of Uganda'. It would involve building up the local economy, but also rebuilding Sudanese systems which would be able to co-exist with the formal and informal Ugandan structures. Integration also implied working very closely with government departments which would eventually take over the role of the agencies.

For UNHCR, however, 'integration' was defined much more narrowly. It did not envisage the settlement being integrated into the broader social and economic context of the county as a whole. Integration was defined strictly in terms of the immediate population living within a radius of six kilometres of the settlement—a definition which was reflected in its funding commitments for local developments.

Self-reliance: There were similar problems over the concept of self-sufficiency: no one was really clear about what it implied. Did it mean sufficiency in terms of food and agricultural production, or did the concept extend to the ability to purchase other essential commodities? Perhaps it meant having a sufficiency measured by the standards of the host population? Or maybe, if those were considered inadequate, 'sufficiency' should be measured by another predetermined criterion? For some, people would only ever be self-sufficient when they could generate enough income to maintain community services like schools, dispensaries, or even government administration. And no one was clear about how far self-reliance would depend on, and therefore extend to, the local population.

For Oxfam in Ikafe, the initial objective was to reach self-reliance in every aspect of the refugees' lives, not just agricultural self-sufficiency. It would ultimately involve the ability to provide (either directly or through taxation) support for social services (health and education) and other welfare services.

Confused commitments

There was never any forum to debate such issues, yet it was these fundamental discrepancies in the definitions of 'integration' and 'self-sufficiency' which increased many of the tensions that affected the programme. The different goals would require very different resources, yet the expectations and capacities of the various agencies to deliver were never clarified or formally agreed.

On the question of withdrawal, time-frames were never clearly established, and there was no agreement on how progress would be measured. It is very unlikely that aggregate indicators could be used for a settlement programme, because refugee communities are usually so stratified. Vulnerable groups needed to be taken into account. How would their needs be assessed? Would it be possible to target these groups? Some protection would still be needed, especially for legal issues and advocacy, after agency presence had been reduced. What did agencies intend to maintain after refugees had apparently attained 'self-sufficiency'?

Reaching agreement on what would be necessary in order to achieve a sustainable settlement was never going to be easy, because of the differing agendas and interpretations of people involved. It needed a considerable degree of understanding and a readiness to compromise.

Communications with the host population

The nature of the tripartite agreements had created much misunderstanding and even competition among the different agencies. From 1996 until the outbreak of insecurity, monthly co-ordination meetings were held, attended by all three implementing agencies, but not UNHCR. Despite Oxfam's lack of authority, many issues were in fact resolved. It was not so easy, however, to facilitate constructive dialogue and reach agreements with the host population.

Most of the grievances of the local population had always been beyond Oxfam's control. Negotiations were carried out months before Oxfam became involved in the programme, and agreements had been reached with little input from those who would be immediately affected. Oxfam then inherited a situation clouded by mistrust and misunderstanding, and was often caught up in the middle of highly political in-fighting.

Inadequate official channels

Since Uganda's political and administrative units have been decentralised, the allocation of authority between County and District levels is often undefined and can be highly sensitive. In Arua, communication between Aringa politicians and District authorities is often poor, and it became considerably worse as the insurgency grew.

Under the tripartite agreement, Oxfam formally communicated information to local people through the District Council and GoU authorities, but local politics created blockages, and important information often did not get through, even though efforts were made to contact local leaders on a regular basis. When there was resentment about dishonoured 'promises', Oxfam was usually the first to get the blame. Staff were invariably seen at the County level to be favouring District interests, while in fact they were trying to operate within the confines of the formal agreement.

The following letter from representatives of the Aringa youth, written in April 1996, illustrates the frustration of the Aringa, who felt ignored, and the kind of tension that arose through lack of dialogue. The letter was handed to an Oxfam driver who was detained by the youth in Yumbe. (Impromptu meetings demanding Oxfam presence were not unusual; and Oxfam vehicles were held on at least two occasions with demands to pay ransoms for their release.)

> ❦ This notice serves to inform you that we, the youths of Aringa, are waiting for you here in Yumbe Resource Centre for the meeting. However, we are very sorry to learn that the meeting is scheduled to take place at Bidibidi. In this regard we, the youths, are not going there plus the political leaders. In addition, those names appeared on the list should pack and go immediately. More so, we want you to abide by our resolutions. If not, there is no way for Oxfam. We are already fed-up. [Signed 'No Thanks'] ❧

Once local representatives were finally brought into the planning process, there was still little opportunity for Oxfam staff to start building bridges with them, because of the pressures to get relief operations under way. Plans were made with very little consultation. Resentment built up as elders and local politicians felt that their authority was being undermined. Ayubu N., an elder, complained in 1997:

> ❦ There were never any formal introductions early on. No one took time to explain the objectives of the programme. There was initially no money given for welcoming ceremonies. We were expecting the refugees through Oxfam to show some appreciation for all that we had given — a small ceremony with a few goats or a bull — but there was never anything given. ❧

Problems with contracts and funding

The awarding of contracts for construction work or provision of building materials was particularly contentious. Oxfam had always been at pains to ensure that any tenders were advertised locally, and that the tendering process was clearly understood by any local contractors. Efforts were made to involve local suppliers of materials such as bricks and wood. Yet Oxfam was obliged to take the most competitive offer. When the Aringa did not win the contracts, the decision was taken as a snub, and tensions increased.

In addition, Oxfam was never really in a position to state unequivocally what it was able to provide in terms of funding for the host population, because the resources depended on a range of other factors, most especially the interests and confidence of donors. Oxfam carried out research to identify local needs, submitted proposals for funding, and was at pains to explain its own constraints to the local population. But local politicians were interested only in seeing tangible results.

Creating space for discussion

By signing the tripartite agreement, Oxfam had to some extent limited its scope for lobbying to create a sound policy environment for successful settlement. Although it did not sign the agreement until after decisions had been taken, Oxfam was still restricted (and to an extent held responsible) by the sheer fact that it was a signatory. This made it extremely difficult to act as an advocate on behalf of the local people to ensure that their rights and wishes were respected.

Yet there were still measures that Oxfam could take, apart from the obvious things such as fund-raising for local infrastructural development. The issue of land rights was extremely important to local leaders, and Oxfam was able to raise awareness by creating a forum in which positions could be clarified, and rights and laws discussed.

The process of the Joint Review, mentioned above, brought local politicians together with representatives from central government, UNHCR, and WFP at the Kampala level, and raised contentious matters such as land rights and compensation. They were able to discuss their different understandings of what 'integration' would imply in practical terms. Although none of the commitments tallied with local expectations, the Review did provide an opportunity for issues to be aired. The process of the Review also gave a chance for refugee leaders to voice concerns over the size of land allocation; and to hear WFP's plans to reduce food relief in the future. If dialogue at this level had been initiated earlier — before Oxfam became involved — matters might not have come to a head as they did.

Towards the end of 1995, regular monthly meetings were set up between the Project Manager, the Local Councils, and elders. These were supposed to be chaired by the Ministry of Local Government (the government department co-ordinating refugee affairs), but were frequently not attended by the representative, which put Oxfam in a difficult position. Although the meetings started late and invariably turned out to be volatile, they were an important starting point in listening to local demands. They helped Oxfam to understand the perspectives of local people better, and ensured that their ideas were taken into consideration. It also put Oxfam in a better position to represent local concerns to government or UNHCR.

Around this time, Oxfam surveyors worked through elders and LC members to clarify boundaries and sacred sites. Demands for land purification were addressed — a token gesture in many ways, but a significant step towards recognising the concerns of local people.

Building alliances between refugees and their hosts

It was essential that alliances were forged between the Sudanese and Ugandan populations, for purposes of social reconstruction and to support local economic development. For the refugee community, interaction with the host communities was important for the further reason that it was seen as a source of security, as a woman refugee in Imvepi explained:

> ❝ The nationals around are the best security. They know what is going on. They are not these gun people; they are just like us. They often came to reassure us last year when things were bad. And when we moved to the transit centre [in Imvepi] last year, they moved with us, and we made sure that they were given *tukuls* for the time they stayed there. ❞

The two communities did inevitably begin to integrate on an informal level, especially through the markets and employment. Many refugees sought piece-rate work in the fields of local farmers. Some approached neighbouring land-lords for land to cultivate. Where tangible services were to be had, there was always a good level of social integration. Local children began to attend the schools in Ikafe; for some it was the first time they had ever gone to classes in Uganda, and it was not unusual to find teenagers studying at very primary levels. In August 1996, for example, 1,538 of the 14,770 children attending schools — over 10 per cent — were Ugandans. The average daily attendance sheets at the Imvepi health centre still show that Ugandans consistently outnumber Sudanese out-patients, by more than four to one in the feeding centres.

Some of the refugee community made their own approaches. According to a group of refugees: *'[In 1995], some Points contributed to buy sheep for nationals to make ceremonies of ritual rites demanded by the Aringa.'* ... '*Now in Imvepi, when there is a funeral, the refugees will get together and send a delegation and some contribution. And it works both ways. The LCs attended a funeral in this Point last month.*' In time, this sort of interaction would probably have fostered the establishment of formal or legal relationships between the two communities. In the event, however, the settlement was disrupted before this could happen, and relations between them remained limited to the very local environment.

It had also been assumed that the parallel refugee and LC administrative structures would automatically foster interaction, and Oxfam had avoided taking too great a lead role, preferring to try to promote refugee capacity. In the event, however, both communities consistently awaited formal introductions, and very few bridges were established until 1995. This increased the refugees' sense of isolation and vulnerability, especially during the insecurity.

Oxfam had hoped to involve the Local (Ugandan) Councils as much as possible in the process of refugee elections, in community meetings, and in any workshops which took place. Yet as staff struggled to meet the everyday needs of the refugee community, there was very little opportunity to develop links. According to the Project Manager, '*For most of the first year, the Community [Officers] functioned more like policemen. They were the interface between those communities who had been left with inadequate infrastructure, or who were suffering because of delays in food. There was very little time for more constructive dialogue.*'

From 1996, Oxfam tried to introduce a better approach to shared resources, which was something that had caused so much friction in the early days. Equal representation for Ugandans and Sudanese was made mandatory on all grinding-mill and water-pump committees; and both communities were involved in the siting of joint infrastructure like schools or health centres. Unfortunately the insecurity hit at about the same time as this process was instituted, which made it difficult to monitor the impact.

Agriculture and health extension work were widened to include local communities within the immediate environment. A Public Health Promoter recalled:

> ❝ We extended our services to people around Yoyo [the central zone of Ikafe]. Refugee extension staff visited the homes of people living within 3–4 kilometres. The first time, we found just two pit latrines. After the second visit, there were ten. It was like an exchange visit; the refugees also gained. ❞

There was never the opportunity, because of the insecurity, to explore opportunities for extending credit and business training opportunities to the local population.

Keeping in touch with refugees

It is important that refugees have adequate information to enable them to make strategic choices. Relaying messages to refugees about food delivery, for example, would help them to plan for delays. Keeping them informed about policy on food rations would enable individual households to monitor whether they were getting their full entitlements. Representation was emphasised precisely because it would give refugees a channel to contribute to planning in an emergency context.

Good communication was even more important as the insecurity took hold, and especially after Oxfam had evacuated most of its staff. Refugees already felt abandoned, and it was vital to let them know that Oxfam was still trying to look after their interests. People felt even less able to control events in such an unstable environment, and information about anything that would affect their lives could help them to plan and make decisions.

Evacuated and out of touch

During Oxfam's enforced partial withdrawal from Ikafe, its absence was perceived by refugees as a lack of interest, even though staff were working full-time from Arua to try to ensure that their basic needs were addressed, and it was often simply impossible to travel the roads into the settlement because of insecurity. In addition, many refugee extension staff, who should have served as a vital link with the community, became even more distanced from them. An old widow complained during the time in Yumbe:

> ❙ The Community Facilitators do not understand our problems; all these "working class" people are the same. They have money to rent homes, and to buy food when it is short ... They do not sleep out in the rains with us here. ❚

It was also inevitable that, because they were not present, staff did not always appreciate the situation of the refugees, or fully understand their needs. A prime example was when the transit at Bidibidi was attacked in February 1997, and seven refugees lost their lives. No one went to offer condolences, and no help was provided for the burial of the dead or the performance of funeral rites. The resulting resentment has been difficult to overcome.

The period of insecurity underlined the importance of being open and consistent with messages, because it helps to build trust. At one time, for example, a refugee community was attacked after staff had been encouraging people to return to their settlements in order to catch the planting season. Again, in October 1997, 18 children were abducted and one lost her life, just days after refugees had been persuaded to move back from the transit area in

Imvepi. Such incidents affected the trust and working relationships between refugees and the agency in the very long term.

Creating channels to communicate over distances

Most of the refugee staff at middle-management levels chose to stay with the displaced refugees during the insecurity and provided a vital link between Oxfam and the community. Many took on new responsibilities for guiding programming, especially in education, community organisation, and land use. These people in many ways enabled Oxfam to maintain its non-urgent operations. According to a group at the workshop in February, *'Leaving the skeleton Ugandan staff and refugee staff in the field has sustained refugees' hopes and expectations'*.

On both occasions when Oxfam was obliged to evacuate its staff, meetings were held with refugee leaders to explain how essential services would be maintained, and what would be done to make sure their concerns were heard by UNHCR and the government in Arua and Kampala. Transport costs and bicycles were supplied to some leaders from Imvepi, which was often particularly inaccessible, in order to help them to reach Arua.

Organisational issues

Improving communication skills

One of the major problems on the Ikafe programme was the fact that technical staff, such as food distributors or land surveyors, had not always undergone training to help them to understand the importance of communicating with and listening to refugees or the host population. As a result, although these people in the field constituted one of the most important interfaces between Oxfam and the host and refugee communities, some of the technical staff did not always prioritise good communication. Even Community Officers who were responsible for integration and representation did not always have the skills to initiate a good level of consultation with either community.

Training in gender-awareness and Oxfam's core values such as participation had been given to all staff in the very early days of the programme, as part of their induction. However, its scope was inevitably limited by the pressures to get the Ikafe settlement up and running. The communication skills of staff in the field were assessed during 1996, and over 130 field staff were given relevant training at the end of that year. In addition, a consultant was brought in to train agricultural staff in PRA skills; and a number of refugees were also trained in participatory research skills. Yet there was never time to follow up the trainings, or before that to monitor staff in the field. The programme was gradually gaining the space to begin to address such challenges when the insecurity hit.

Staffing

Oxfam went some way to improving dialogue with the local population by appointing local people to three out of the five Community Officer positions. This ensured that a local perspective was kept central to planning, and that there were informal as well as formal channels for voicing concerns, especially over issues such as violations of sacred sites, or problems over shared resources. However, it was never enough.

Oxfam became increasingly caught up in disputes which would have been better resolved by local official representatives; in response, it considered the idea of employing someone in a liaison capacity who represented Ugandan administrative and political interests, as a way of improving communications. Initially suggested by the MoLG in Ikafe, this was a highly sensitive political issue at the time, so it was not possible to follow it up. Yet having somebody to explain Oxfam's position on issues such as awarding of contracts, siting of infrastructure, or equal employment opportunities might have helped to reduce some of the tensions which built up with local politicians.

It could be argued that Oxfam should have appointed a 'Communications Officer' for the Ikafe programme. It was important to ensure that communications work was prioritised, yet there was always a danger that, like gender work, policy work, or social research, communications work would be marginalised if all the responsibility was given to one person. There was also the problem of where to position a Communications Officer so that he or she would have sufficient influence to ensure that issues were taken up. The LCs and other local bodies, as well as the refugees' representatives, wanted to negotiate with people who could take hard decisions. They needed to have confidence in whoever was to be the interface between themselves and Oxfam.

Another part of the work of a Communications Officer, if appointed, would have been to act as the link with donors and official visitors, and to assist in the production of reports to donors and potential funders. Yet an equally important aspect would be to improve communication techniques in the field, through training and the production of extension materials; and to identify and work to remove obstacles where there was poor communication going on. Oxfam found it extremely difficult to find one individual to fulfil all these different roles, and although somebody was recruited for a short time in 1996, the Officer's role and position within the organisation were never very clear.

Advocacy work

For Oxfam, influencing policy is a core part of any programme activity. Development activities, emergency operations, and advocacy on behalf of marginalised communities are integrated into a single programme of work; this is known as the 'one programme' approach. In Ikafe, Oxfam managers were involved in trying to influence the decisions of central and local government, UNHCR, and WFP on a number of issues. A significant amount of time was spent in the early days trying to slow down the rate at which refugees were transferred, and insisting on the provision of adequate infrastructure before people were moved. Later on, when insecurity increased, appeals were made to the Ugandan authorities, through UNHCR and directly to MoLG, to improve protection for the refugees and agency staff within the settlement. There were also long disputes with UNHCR over the size of agricultural plots, and hence the carrying capacity of the settlement; and requests for improved supplies of non-food items, to prevent Oxfam having to ask families to share with other families. Appeals were also made to WFP to improve the timing of food deliveries and to create buffer stocks.

Tensions

Lobbying work inevitably creates tensions, especially when the agencies concerned have conflicting objectives. In Ikafe, the challenge for Oxfam was to try to understand the constraints under which others were operating, without compromising its commitment to its own core values in the matter of refugee rights.

There was always the risk of upsetting either the GoU or UNHCR, from whom Oxfam's mandate derived. In any situation, an agency can only ever function at the discretion of the host government. Marring relations with the government on a particularly sensitive issue might have affected the agency's ability to operate in other parts of Uganda, and poor relations with UNHCR could have threatened Oxfam's ability to work in other refugee situations.

Tension between Oxfam and UNHCR centred initially on the speed of the first refugee transfers. It had been a high-level government decision to transfer the refugees at very short notice, and UNHCR was under considerable pressure from government to help to disband the border camps in Koboko as quickly as possible, and to cope with growing refugee numbers. To some extent, UNHCR's hands were tied, and there appeared to be very little room for manoeuvre. Yet Oxfam still felt that UNHCR could have done more on humanitarian grounds to try to persuade the government to slow the transfers. Despite a reluctance to jeopardise its position as implementing partner by appearing in the eyes of UNHCR to have exceeded its mandate, Oxfam felt it necessary to try to influence the decision. According to the Country Representative: *'Our main concern was to maintain humanitarian efforts, rather than complain and withdraw. From previous experience we had seen that the Government of Uganda had moved refugees for reasons of national security, without thought for humanitarian concerns.'*

In the event, because of its insistent lobbying on humanitarian grounds against rapid transfers, Oxfam was accused by UNHCR of exceeding its mandate, and its position as an implementing partner in Ikafe was seriously questioned by UNHCR as early as December 1994.

When rebel activity was at its most intense, Oxfam felt compelled to lobby government through UNHCR for an improvement in the security situation. There was a strong response from Kampala, indicating the extreme sensitivity of the situation. Oxfam was accused of casting a slur on the GoU's concern for the plight of refugees, and of calculating to mar the good relations between government, UNHCR, and its partners.

The tripartite agreement between the Ministry of Local Government (MoLG) and UNHCR had an impact on Oxfam's scope for action. By giving agencies individual responsibilities for certain aspects of the programme — UNHCR for protection, government for security and administration of refugee affairs, and Oxfam for implementation of relief activities — the agreement in some ways restricted the spheres in which Oxfam could try to influence policy decisions.

At one time, the government did not want to promote refugee settlement or camping outside the area gazetted for that purpose — an area from which refugees had fled in fear of their lives. Oxfam was afraid that parts of the Ikafe settlement were still liable to rebel attack. Lobbying on security issues was not part of Oxfam's official mandate as an implementing partner; yet the remaining refugees were suffering terribly, and members of the Oxfam staff were having to cope with the anger and frustration that was being projected on to them.

Finding a balance

An international agency is ultimately operating in a foreign land, and there may be limits to what it can or should lobby to change. It is perhaps true that foreign organisations are in a powerful position, because they can say certain things that local people cannot, but there are strong moral and political arguments which question the right of foreigners to interfere at all.

On the other hand, Oxfam is committed to certain basic principles, which it felt compelled to uphold in Ikafe. For example, Oxfam lobbied the GoU to allow distributions outside the settlement to refugees displaced in Yumbe, on behalf of children, pregnant mothers, and the elderly, who were being asked to walk over 20 kilometres along unsafe roads to carry a 15-day ration of food. Some were choosing not to go to collect their food, because they were physically unable, too weak, or afraid of being attacked by armed bandits on rebels on the roads. Roda A. complained:

> ❦ A young girl of 13 years was abducted and raped while walking from Bidibidi to Yumbe in February. How can I send my children to pick up food there when the road is so unsafe? But I will not make the distance because of my [heavily pregnant] condition, and my husband is already in the Sudan. ❧

Joyce G. described her dilemma as follows:

> ❦ I was raped by six people [allegedly rebels] on the Koboko road last August. They lined up to take me. By that time I was already three months pregnant. Then when [my Point] was attacked in November, I ran back to save my things before the house was burned, and seven more raped me there. My husband is in Sudan, and I have seven other children all under 18 years. The oldest ones are girls. I cannot send them to collect food when the road is not safe, but we are suffering hunger, so what to do? ❧

This woman gave birth to a child shortly afterwards, in the open under a mango tree. The child survived only one day: the mother had no breast-milk and was officially ineligible for any agency support, because she was not within the settlement area.

On this occasion, the government responded very positively to Oxfam's requests, and a one-off humanitarian distribution was permitted. The government was understandably concerned to contain refugees within an area where it felt it could better guarantee the refugees' security. It was also responding to local concerns, as refugee numbers swelled in the towns, and there were fears about the threat of disease in heavily overcrowded camps. This was one of many times when the government responded positively to Oxfam's lobbying work, especially to increase the presence of security forces within the settlement area.

It is worth noting that speaking out on contentious issues in Ikafe helped to build up the confidence and understanding of staff. It also strengthened the relationship between Oxfam and the refugees.

Getting the right balance between lobbying on a sensitive issue and being permitted to continue its operations ultimately requires any agency to establish a bottom line, especially for organisations concerned with human rights (as opposed to those providing exclusively humanitarian assistance). At times it may be better to withdraw completely in order to expose a problem, rather than to compromise — but that is usually a last resort. In the case of Ikafe, the dilemmas were rarely so extreme.

The politics of funding

An organisation's power to lobby is influenced by a number of factors: its reputation and track record in the country in question, for example, the contacts it has managed to develop, and the support it can attract from other networks and alliances. In many cases, an agency's capacity to influence major matters of policy may be linked to its funding base. Self-funding agencies make attractive partners for UNHCR — but one with its own sources of income inevitably has a greater capacity to bargain than one which does not. In Ikafe, Oxfam was initially able to raise funds from a variety of sources, and was therefore more valuable to UNHCR as an implementing agency—while at the same time being in a stronger position to influence policy decisions.

When an organisation depends on just one source of funding, it is much more difficult for it to remain flexible. Later on, as funding shortages became a problem for Oxfam, the balance of power shifted. It was much harder to lobby on fundamental issues, like programme priorities or the provision of particular in-puts which Oxfam considered necessary, when funding depended to such a great extent on the very organisation it was trying to influence.

Identifying other strengths

For agencies which do not have the luxury of a good funding base, there are other strengths that can be built upon. Referring to some of the protocols, especially those of the UN agencies, and to UN Conventions, helped Oxfam to lobby more effectively in Ikafe. Claims could also be based on the WFP/UNHCR Memorandum of Understanding, which specifically defines their respective responsibilities. UNHCR is responsible for ensuring protection of refugees; WFP has certain policies of good practice, formulated in Rome and guaranteed in writing; governments have an interest in presenting a good image on the world stage, especially in respect of human rights.

Oxfam also has its own set of principles, which staff in the field found helpful for reference. The organisation's commitment to the concept of 'Basic Rights', for example, provided a useful baseline for lobbying work. It meant that, when staff in the field felt that refugees' basic rights were being undermined, staff at various levels were more confident to argue their point.

Careful and credible research is also vital to lobbying initiatives. Documenting the experiences of refugees can help donors to understand the impact of practices such as late food delivery or poor allocation of non-food items. Even if the practices are beyond the immediate control of agencies concerned, focusing attention on the issues can help to prevent something similar happening in the future.

Sound analysis and accurate information are the key to doing good policy work. Ikafe had the luxury of two full-time researchers, responsible for collecting data direct from the field. While much of this research was geared to the improvement of programming work, issues inevitably emerged which would be relevant to policy advisers. These could be used by staff in the relevant sectors to communicate the reality of life in Ikafe to those who were making decisions. Case studies and verbatim testimony are a good way of illustrating the human impact of policies formulated at a distance.

Oxfam always tried to ensure that refugee leaders were involved in lobbying work in Ikafe. On a number of occasions, transport was provided to bring refugee leaders to meet key people in Arua, especially during the insecurity. This was greatly valued by the displaced communities, who often felt abandoned and powerless. The process of the participatory Joint Review also brought together many different interests, and enabled the voices of the refugees to be heard.

Building alliances

Many decisions about policy are made at the headquarters of international organisations, and changes may create precedents which have repercussions in other situations. In such cases, it is often more productive to try to influence decisions informally. Some strategic programme decisions can still be made at the local level. Solutions to immediate problems often depend on the attitudes of agency staff on the ground, and their relationships with UNHCR, WFP, or government representatives. When WFP allowed Oxfam to distribute food inside the Ikafe settlement without a full complement of staff on the ground, the decision was made on the basis of the good level of understanding which had been achieved in the field.

Oxfam staff found it helpful in Ikafe to build alliances with a number of key people, especially in government. A number of officials who were responsible for refugees at District level were funded by Oxfam to attend a course at the Refugee Studies Programme in the UK. This initiative helped to enhance understanding among relevant authorities of the kinds of issues with which Oxfam was concerned in Ikafe.

In summary, work needs to be carried out at every level, and in different ways — both formally and informally. In the words of the Country Representative: *'Oxfam must lobby at all levels — international, national, and local. We should be lobbying all the time as we interact with all actors at different levels.'*

In Ikafe, having the support of the Kampala office helped enormously. Staff working on the Ikafe programme were able to highlight the impact of decisions which had been made a long way off, and Kampala staff were then able to raise the matter with the central authorities. On issues with longer-term significance, it may be more appropriate to do lobbying work at an international level. Staff in Oxfam's head office in Oxford, for example, discussed food-distribution mechanisms directly with WFP in Rome.

It may be useful to identify problems that are shared by other programmes, so that a more strategic approach can be developed for advocacy work on programming issues. Cross-programme learning is an important way of identifying similar concerns, particularly within a region.

Where does advocacy work fit in?

An agency getting involved in a programme of this size and complexity has to decide in advance how far it is prepared to go in lobbying for change if it feels that its objectives are being undermined. Advocacy work is fundamental to Oxfam's 'One Programme' approach, which incorporates relief, development, and policy work into all project activities. In the view of the Country Representative, in Uganda *'lobbying, as a matter of routine, is a key role for all senior managers and policy analysts'*.

Employing someone specifically for lobbying work runs the risk of separating policy work from programming, and creating confusion. However, it is equally important that people at a senior level are committed to ensuring that influencing work on key policy issues is kept on the agenda, and that relevant information is gathered. In Ikafe, it was useful to have funding for the Research and Policy Team that was entirely independent of UNHCR or other major donors, because it meant that Oxfam was able to retain a degree of autonomy in its influencing work.

Advocacy work is never easy. There will always be areas where relations between the main players are marred; and others where an agency feels that more could have been done. There are no right or wrong answers, but thinking through in advance some of the implications of doing policy work, and giving support to field staff so that they have mechanisms to express their concerns, are important starting points.

Organisational issues 7

The quality of support which Oxfam was able to provide in Ikafe depended on having high-calibre staff who had sufficient understanding to take on a project of such diversity, and good systems of resource management which would enable the programme to adapt to an ever-changing situation. This chapter considers some of the organisational aspects of the programme, especially related to systems for resource management.

Working in situations like Ikafe puts enormous strain on an agency's management systems. Yet many of the emergencies in the 1990s demanded programmes of the scale and complexity of Ikafe. The crisis in the Great Lakes region of Africa makes Ikafe pale almost into insignificance. The demands now placed on humanitarian organisations trying to respond to such crises have become almost the 'norm' at the present time, and agencies consequently need to create systems which will enable them to respond effectively.

For Oxfam's head office in the UK, the Ikafe programme posed complex organisational problems, in terms of structures, staff, finance, vehicles, and logistics, and particular challenges in the areas of planning, funding, and administrative support. It was also a great drain on the time of many people in the UK: emergency staff, fund-raisers, and the regional desk; and it absorbed a huge amount of money: half of Oxfam's Catastrophe Fund was used up in just one financial year.

Ikafe and Imvepi together employed a staff of 145 contracted Ugandans at the height of activities in December 1996, over 142 refugees on incentive, and a further 9 Ugandan staff on secondment from the District Medical Office. There were similar numbers of loaders, cleaners, and skilled crafts people, continuously employed on a casual basis. It created a huge imbalance in Oxfam's Uganda programme, because substantial resources, including human resources, were diverted to a single area. Oxfam's operations in Uganda expanded from a staff of 30 to over 160, while the annual budget expanded from £1 million to over £4 million. There were some positive gains: financial and logistics systems were streamlined in Uganda, higher-calibre support staff were taken on, and people acquired wider experience which is already being put to use in new areas of conflict within Uganda. But overall, the programme taxed Oxfam as an organisation very severely.

Oxfam's development programmes tend to be small, and its support not geared to large-scale implementation. Emergencies, on the other hand, are usually short-term, with different systems and specific time-bound funding. Ikafe fell somewhere between the two — as have Oxfam's responses in Sudan, Afghanistan, Sri Lanka, and many other complex emergency situations. Although emergency-support staff were brought in from Oxford to provide the necessary managerial and logistical support, the systems which they put in place proved to be relevant in the short term only, because of the dynamic nature of the programme. When gaps became evident, there was often not the time or capacity to think about filling them.

Planning and funding

Flexible planning cycles

In many ways, the need for speed resulted in a lack of realism when the programme was being developed in Ikafe. A manager in Oxfam House recalls:

> ❦ There was an awful lot of jargon being bandied about.
> The original project proposal was almost a case of "How many buzz words can we fit into one sentence?" We were all talking about things like "a developmental approach to emergency work", and sustainability. Maybe if we had not been so caught up in the jargon and with selling the idea, we could have looked at what was really feasible. ❞

As a result, the original objectives were over-ambitious. Self-reliance was to be attained within a certain time-frame, yet there had never been the time or space to identify whether it was really feasible on the basis of the physical conditions on the ground.

The programme in Ikafe remained essentially an emergency operation. As early as 1994, UNHCR was threatening to withdraw aid and bring in another agency; the uncertainty continued through 1995, and then the project was thrown into insecurity for most of 1996 and 1997. There was never any breathing space, and time was always a factor. New refugee arrivals were constantly expected, yet the debate about carrying capacity remained unresolved — two years into the programme. In retrospect it could be argued that the objectives should have been modified; another manager in Oxfam House has suggested that *'assisting individual households to partially develop plots'* would have been more realistic.

There were no management systems to ring alarm bells when it became obvious that, in the context at that time, the programme could not achieve its set objectives. Until the Review in 1996, there was never any space to allow a proper re-appraisal of what the programme could offer. In the opinion of a manager in the Emergencies Department:

> ❟ A successful programme is all about having realistic objectives and then being able to monitor the work against those. Staff involved need to be able to take a reality check every now and then. Where objectives cannot be met, then it needs to be made explicit and the programme and activities readapted. ❜

Without a proper understanding of the context and constraints within which the programme is operating, there is a danger that activities are carried out on an *ad hoc* basis, and a programme begins to drift. In such an unstable environment as Ikafe, where the stakes were constantly changing, it needed to be done on a regular basis. As another manager in Ikafe put it:

> ❟ We call it the "Frog in the Water syndrome". The water builds up so gradually that no one notices until it is too late. Systems for planning need to be live documents, not a single project proposal that is hardly opened up again, once it has been signed off. ❜

Once it is recognised that some of the goals are not attainable, a proper assessment can be made of the compromises and difficult choices which may have to be made. An emergency situation like Ikafe, where speed and uncertainty are the overriding factors, requires flexible planning, regular reviews, and input from outsiders to keep it on course.

Measuring impact

Even if the objectives had been more realistic, with so many different donors involved there would still have been differing opinions about how to measure the impact of the programme.

For WFP, for example, self-reliance would be gauged by crop assessments; UNHCR might want to add assessments of progress towards self-financed provision of health care and education, and community services such as water points and grinding mills. Oxfam would ideally go a step further and examine how different aspects of the project had contributed to the empowerment and capacity-building of refugees, in social, economic, or political terms; and how far the local economy and society had developed so that the refugee and host communities were living side by side in a sustainable way. In a Briefing Paper written in 1995, a year after the programme was conceived, the Emergencies Manager wrote:

> ❟ Indeed, the definition of self-sufficiency is highly complex. Which criteria do we use — income, assets, access to services? What do we compare it with — the local people, the previous Sudanese lifestyle?

What indeed do the Sudanese want, given that most will probably
want to return home? **,**

For Oxfam, it was difficult to break down the concept of 'self-reliance' into
measurable indicators without consulting a range of groups within the two
communities. But it was hard to get other donors like UNHCR or WFP to
accept that, taken in isolation, quantifiable and pre-defined indicators
represented nothing more than externally determined standards of living.
Using aggregate indicators would probably not accommodate the very
different needs of the more vulnerable people. Impact needed to be measured
in a way which would take into account the huge diversity within the
settlement.

Monitoring with stakeholders
By adopting an action-research approach to the collection of information, and
using research to identify relevant indicators and measure impact on a
continuous basis, Oxfam had always hoped to include the views of both the
host and refugee communities in the process of planning and monitoring. Yet
Ikafe was always so uncertain, and agencies were struggling for much of the
time to meet even the basic needs of the refugees, that people's less urgent
priorities were sometimes overshadowed by immediate concerns — water,
food or security. It was difficult to foster the involvement of refugees and local
people in developing mechanisms for longer-term change.

In 1996, a more participatory approach had been adopted to evaluate and
re-focus the programme. It involved representatives of all the major
stakeholders: the host population, refugees, UNHCR, WFP, the government,
and Oxfam. A series of qualitative indicators was developed, which were later
refined through participatory research. They included the degree to which
labour was being sold to local Ugandans in return for food, as a measure of
food security; the number of children staying on in school classes for a whole
day, rather than leaving early because they were hungry or had other domestic
responsibilities; changes in diets (being able to afford to drink coffee, for
example, or purchase goat meat). Having the time to sit around a fire at night
and tell stories was another suggestion put forward to measure how far
households had regained control over their lives, and felt that a degree of
security had returned.[1] Such features of settlement life were to be measured
periodically, using various tools of participatory rural appraisal (PRA).
Although attempts were made to put qualitative indicators into workplans for
1997, the insecurity meant that they were never relevant. In addition, they
were difficult to use, because other groups had a different set of goal posts (few
of which had been agreed upon).

Obstacles to community involvement

Agencies which embark on operational 'development' programmes usually expect to have the time to identify the context and plan in advance, in collaboration with the community. Some longer-term capacity-building projects have a ten-year time-frame, the first year of which may be spent carrying out socio-political and economic analyses, often through PRA exercises, then ensuring funding, recruiting and training the right staff, and generally gearing up for implementation of the plans. In Ikafe, there was no time for such luxuries. Everything came at once. There was never much space at the outset or later on, especially as security declined, even for consultation with communities. As a result, the process of planning in Ikafe remained much more top–down than managers would have liked.

The constant revisions to the budget accentuated this process. As the programme became more and more dependent on UNHCR for funding, managers were increasingly constrained by the need to be seen to perform in tangible terms, defined by the donors. It did not help to create the space for a more participatory approach to planning.

There was less space than ever to explore more radical ways of working with communities. UNHCR was demanding budget forecasts long before staff on the ground had had any opportunity to think creatively about planning for the year ahead. In consequence, budgets were more or less created by an accountant who rarely visited the field and may not have had a proper understanding of programme needs. Staff on the ground later found themselves doing workplans for the following year on the basis of pre-determined budgets, with very little room for any creative participation of communities. Similar problems arose as a result of constant revisions of the UNHCR budget: funds were cut, and staff were unable to carry out planned activities. A member of staff in Ikafe complained: '*Whenever we need something urgently, like fuel to pump water to refugees, or a small spare part for a vehicle, there is always the same response: "Where is the budget?"'*

Financial support and control

Funds for the Ikafe budget, which reached over £3 million at one time, excluding food and other goods in kind, came from nine different donors. Budgets of this size are easily handled in a single-sector programme with straightforward accounting. But Ikafe was a multi-sector *and* multi-donor programme. It needed extremely good accounting systems to accommodate the different requirements of donors, and to ensure tight control of expenditure.

Oxfam systems tend not to be geared to large-scale operational projects, and proper monitoring of expenditure at different levels was often impossible. An accountant was seconded to the programme full-time for six months in 1995 to ensure good resource-management, and then again in 1996. Yet, however good the systems, they depended on having the right person permanently in place to monitor and maintain them. It was difficult to find good accountants who were prepared to work in a situation like Ikafe, so much of the accounting had to be done in Kampala, which did not allow for proper financial management at the project level. Ikafe over-spent and had to be bailed out by Oxfam House on several occasions, which was not easy.

The very nature and structure of multi-sectoral programmes like Ikafe inevitably incur a more costly staff portfolio than single-sector work, because of the need to have a number of technical and qualified people at senior levels. For example, a single-sector programme is likely to have a small number of senior, qualified staff (such as water technicians or doctors), working with a much larger group of staff with more general skills (like distribution monitors, or casual labourers). The range of skills required across a multi-sectoral programme requires a much larger group of middle- to senior-level staff, who are of course more expensive to employ. This changes the whole staffing profile and consequently the costings.

Another problem for Oxfam in Ikafe was that it often found itself responsible for paying a sizeable proportion of staff salaries. UNHCR has its own funding constraints and has certain policies regarding salary payments which are uniform across Uganda. For the programme's integrity it was important that staff were paid according to salaries which Oxfam deemed fair, and that there was equity and uniformity in salary structures across the country. However, this inevitably meant that Oxfam had to raise large funds for administration, which is always unattractive to donors.

Overcoming funding difficulties

Long-term support in an unstable refugee context is extremely difficult, and cannot be guaranteed. But that is not a good enough reason to ignore the need to respond. Fund-raisers and managers in Kampala and Oxfam House spent much time in trying to lobby donors to support long-term measures. Individual proposals to fund different aspects of the programme, particularly local development activities, were continually put to different donors, but with limited success.

In the early stages, funding was much less of a problem: donors often respond positively to calls for relief aid, and Ikafe was no exception. It was later on, especially in 1996, that funding for longer-term measures proved difficult. Some limited finance was raised through the European Union for local rehabilitation work, but few donors have such budget lines. Donors were tired of the protracted Sudanese situation, and the area was increasingly unstable. Oxfam was appealing for funds to help refugees to develop, while — as the donors saw it — they would all one day (and probably soon) leave the area entirely, so what was the point? Ikafe was soon facing serious shortages of funds, and a black cloud hung over the programme for most of 1996 and into 1997. Being over-dependent on one donor meant that managers often lost the freedom to develop the programme in the way that they would have chosen.

Accepting uncertainty

In situations like Ikafe, agencies serious about meeting objectives need to be realistic about what they are getting into. They need to ask themselves if they have the capacity to provide the level of support needed, in finance, logistics, or management systems. Have they considered all the implications? Are they really prepared to make a commitment of funding and organisational support for a period of three to five years?

They need to understand what is involved, and have systems for continuously monitoring change. It is unfair to ask staff to embark on activities which then fall prey to budget revisions. But they also need financial systems that are flexible enough to accommodate the uncertain and changing environment in which the project is being implemented. In Ikafe this meant, in the words of the Country Representative, the ability to *'accept uncertainty in an organised way'*.

Management structures

The Ikafe programme needed an integrated approach which would ensure that in every activity staff took account of the fact that livelihoods consist of a whole of range of factors, and that activities in one sphere would have an impact on another.

Ikafe was initially set up on functional lines to run an emergency programme, with elements largely pre-identified and planned by Oxfam. Yet the intention was always to move towards a community-based programme, and, as such, the activities of different sectors needed to be integrated right from the start. For example, if construction had been more closely linked with community development, it would have been much easier to promote voluntary contributions, and to put systems in place for roads maintenance. Problems over plot allocation and site boundaries might have been better resolved with the involvement of the people responsible for community representation. Surveyors need to have good interpersonal skills, because land is such a contentious issue for the host population. It was always hard to decide where to fit the research and policy team, in order to ensure that lessons were turned into action.

Structures needed to be redesigned to enable the programme to meet its aims. Three teams were created — for Land Use, Community Organisation, and Public Health — which enabled a much more integrated approach. Realising that extension workers are also crucial to the process of integration, Oxfam now holds workshops twice a month in Imvepi to help extension staff work together better. Initially these became a battleground, with each sector accusing the other of disrupting their activities. Now, as a Community Facilitator reflects:

> ❪ It is so much easier to carry out my work. In the Points I am responsible for, we meet as a small team — myself, with the Community Health Worker and Agro-forestry person. Then if we are to hold a meeting, we all attend and help each other. We never realised before how much one thing affects another. ❫

It was always important to ensure that sectoral issues, such as sound environmental practice, featured on the agendas of other Teams. Managers at different levels needed to have the leverage to ensure that their sectoral concerns were accounted for in other activities. More broad-based concerns such as gender and social policy are also likely to get forgotten or seen as a luxury when the people responsible are not positioned to enable them to make changes.

The physical layout of the Ikafe settlement created problems for the adoption of an integrated approach to its development. Ikafe was divided into four zones, with Imvepi forming the fifth. Each was effectively like a small project in its own right, supporting between 7,000 and 11,000 refugees. Yet sectors were still managed and run from the central base in Bidibidi, which made some of the other zones feel marginalised. Having a management structure based on sectors, as opposed to one which integrated different sectors in a particular physical area, or at least unified sectors under various teams, did not facilitate effective co-ordination and integration of activities at the Zonal level, or always promote links between various activities. Yet Ikafe was never in a position to move to a fully integrated (zonal) approach, which would have meant that every zone functioned effectively as a mini-project. Those sectors concerned with basic needs, like distribution and water, continued to require a sectoral structure. As a compromise, Zonal co-ordinators were created to co-ordinate activities between different sectors, but it increased their work burdens considerably, and successful integration was very dependent on the commitment of individual personalities.

Human resources

The success of any management systems for Ikafe would always depend on how they were interpreted by staff on the ground. The Corporate Finance Manager in Oxford commented: *'It is no good having good systems if you do not have the right managers in place. Someone with the right sort of skills will have the vision to remain flexible. Rigid adherence to financial rules is important, but one must not lose sight of the vision and principles of the programme.'*

Yet good staff were always hard to find. As we have seen throughout this casebook, many of the problems in Ikafe were exacerbated because staff were often not able to cope with such a changeable programme. Getting the right people into Ikafe was always an uphill battle.

People with 'people skills'

Programmes like Ikafe, which are seeking to build capacity at the same time as ensuring basic needs, may attract practitioners from opposite ends of the spectrum. This means that, while there is a wealth of experience and a wide diversity of ideas, there may also be contradictions in the actual implementation of activities.

In the very early days, Ikafe needed technical people with considerable experience of working in emergencies, and staff with the capacity to ensure tangible output at very short notice. Yet Oxfam's vision was eventually to build up community capacity by providing services in a way that respected refugees' own capabilities, and helped them to develop their own skills and mechanisms. This was inevitably a slower process, which needed staff with good interpersonal skills.

A Public Health Promoter has illustrated some of the implications of not getting the balance right initially:

 ❹ We really created some of our problems, because we did not always think ahead enough. In the early days of Ikafe, we paid the youth to dig communal pit latrines for the new settlements. The place was stinking ... Later on, when people were displaced into the transits and we needed them again, there was no budget. And yet they refused completely. One group of youths said to me once: "Why should we dig, when you must be pocketing the money Oxfam has for latrines?" ❺

Operational capacity-building work, carried out alongside the relief of immediate needs, requires a particular approach: a set of values and a way of thinking that puts people first. It needed people who could emphasise the importance of communicating and creating awareness within the community right from the start. Ikafe showed how important it is to have staff at higher management levels, regardless of professional background, who have a solid understanding of 'development' practice, and the ability to incorporate it into relief activities from the outset.

Complex emergencies in particular, where the situation is ever-changing and highly politicised, demand an even higher calibre of staff, with skills to assess and manage highly-charged situations. In Ikafe, conditions were never really stable, and managing the programme meant working against the odds to create or facilitate the elusive 'enabling environment'. It needed people who could remain flexible, and maintain some sort of vision to build on opportunities.

Attracting high-calibre staff

It was extremely difficult to find well-qualified Ugandans who wanted to work in the bush in a remote region which is often unstable. People in the southern and western Districts of Uganda consider Arua to be a harsh and insecure District, and for much of the time Ikafe was not an easy situation, and never conducive to family life. The Administrator in Ikafe explained:

> ❝ People prefer to work in urban centres. The managers mostly came in from other Districts. When they went on leave, they would hardly stay for one week; then it may be another two months in the bush. So there were high drop-off levels. People found they could get better conditions elsewhere, where they could be close to their families. ❞

In the early days, people lived in tents and worked very long hours. The area was infested with poisonous snakes and scorpions. Employment opportunities for wives and husbands outside the three NGOs operating there were very limited; and schooling could not compare with the facilities in urban centres. Then the settlement was beset by insecurity, and families accompanying staff were the first to be evacuated.

Positions in such environments are more attractive to single people (of either sex), who are at a particular stage of their life-cycle where they can afford the risks of travelling to such remote areas. For men or women with many responsibilities, it is often simply not possible. (For many of those who did join and left their families at home, concern for their loved ones was a constant source of stress.)

Training and support

Recruiting the right people is not a matter of making choices between 'people with a development background' and those with experience in relief work. Oxfam's general commitment to a 'one-programme' approach, and the circumstances of the Ikafe programme in particular, implied the need to find staff with the ability to combine relief, development, and advocacy skills in their daily work. More specifically, Ikafe needed staff who combined social and political awareness with technical skills, an understanding of 'development' and capacity-building, a commitment to participatory ways of working, and a sensitivity to gender-related issues and to environmental matters. In the view of one manager: *'It is arguably easier to train people in logistics systems and distribution mechanisms than it is to change their way of thinking, approach or values.'*

Ideally, criteria such as an understanding of gender, or a commitment to capacity-building or participatory approaches, would have been formally incorporated into job descriptions. Yet, as the same manager put it: *'Firstly, speed usually limits quality recruitment and inductions, and second, we tend to focus on the hard skills rather than the people skills in selecting staff'*. In an unattractive working environment, where a high level of technical expertise (in fields like engineering, health, agro-forestry) was required at very short notice, 'people skills' were not always the priority.

In such situations, an agency responsible for a programme on the scale of Ikafe may be tempted to put aside good objectives to recruit locally or to up-grade existing national staff, if this might mean putting operations at risk. In Ikafe, Oxfam had problems filling at least three higher management positions through local recruitment, and in the end resorted to recruiting inter-nationally, which is more costly and can be politically difficult.

People from outside may bring wider experience and knowledge, and they may also have a better understanding of international donors' standards for reporting or accounting. But local staff understand better how local systems and cultures operate; their ways of communication may be more relevant. And there are strong arguments for creating opportunities for building up local capacity and employment. A balance is needed. According to the Country Representative: *'Maybe we need to be more pragmatic and admit that it is difficult to get perfection. There are many advantages to having staff who may have two-thirds of the required skills and experience, but who know Oxfam and have commitment and loyalty.'* What such staff need is the time and support to develop the additional skills.

Training and up-grading of staff became essential in Ikafe. Many of the staff imported from outside the area were well-versed in relief work, but had limited understanding of what capacity-building would really involve. Workshops were held with all those first recruited, as part of their induction, to introduce concepts of gender and community-based approaches, and sensitise staff to some of the particular problems of working with refugees. Later on, it was the pressures of work, rather than poor intentions, which meant that these training sessions were rarely long enough and were never properly followed up.

In emergencies it is very difficult to address training needs alongside the need to deliver services. Yet if a settlement process is to work, the lead agency must prioritise the development of skills which will support communities in rebuilding their lives. One short-term solution to recruitment problems, especially for positions like accountants, is to explore (voluntary) international or national professional secondments. There is always the risk that short-term postings will result in a lack of continuity. However, in the ever-changing environment of Ikafe, where systems needed to be flexible and people prepared to adapt, fresh ideas could bring benefits. Staff tend to 'burn out' more quickly in a situation where plans are consistently being frustrated, or budgets revised, in a context of extreme insecurity. Short-term secondments may enable the programme to remain more responsive and dynamic.

The 'gender question'

Emergency programmes tend to be very male environments. This is partly because the severe conditions do not attract women employees, and posts are rarely 'accompanied'. But if an agency employs only a few women, and those mostly at lower management levels, it is far less likely that concerns about gender will be addressed. Moreover, the agency will create the inadvertent impression that women are not really valued as capable managers. A consultant reporting for Oxfam Uganda commented: '*Had the programme been able to engage a larger number of women staff, they may have been more effective in promoting equality of representation. "Do as we say, not as we do" is rarely an effective strategy for transformation.*'

It was always difficult to attract female staff to the Ikafe programme, especially at upper management levels. Even at the height of activities, women never occupied more than 20 per cent of all posts, with the exception of health staff who were seconded from the District Medical Office and therefore paid on an incentive. Numbers of female staff in the health sector were much higher. For example, in August 1996, of a total health staff of 18 (Ugandans and refugees), twelve (67 per cent) were women. The ratios were also better at the lower grades, although not for typically male activities such as driving, where for 1995 and 1996 there was only one woman driver out of 21. The lack of women drivers reflects cultural preferences for particular jobs, but if Oxfam had tried more actively to recruit women drivers, this might have gone some way to bring about changes in people's perceptions and attitudes. The fact that Oxfam had one woman driver at least was often noted by outsiders. The proportions of women in selected posts in August 1996 are shown in Table 1. For refugee extension staff, figures were similar, as Table 2 shows.

Table 1: Proportions of women staff in selected positions (August 1996)

Grade 8:	Senior Management	0%
Grade 7:	Team Leaders	50%
Grade 6/5:	Programme Co-ordinators	17%
Grade 6/5:	Public Health Promoters	20%
Grade 4/3:	Food Distribution Monitors	40%
Grade 4/3:	Registration Clerks	50%
Grade 4/3:	Administration Staff	80%
Grade 2/1:	Kitchen Staff	100%

Table 2: Proportions of female staff on incentives in selected posts (August 1996)

Refugee Co-ordinators	0%
Extension Workers	
– Community Devt.	19%
– Agro-Forestry	7%
– Public Health (Ikafe)	13%
– Health (Imvepi)	40%
DMO Seconded Health	67%

What was holding women back? It was often difficult for them to take advantage of job opportunities in what was considered an inhospitable environment, when they had families and young children to look after. Schooling, though available, was never comparable with that in urban centres like Kampala. Many said their husbands were reluctant to let them work in Ikafe, and one or two men even forced their wives to resign, because they considered it too insecure. One woman who chose to leave the programme commented:

> ❛ It is easier for men to live in harsh situations, away from their families. Women may be breast-feeding; they may be responsible for young children who cannot run around freely, because of the scorpions and snakes; and later on there is no chance for schooling. Men often do not cherish the idea of their wives working away like that. ❜

Following the insecurity it was even harder. The three women Programme Co-ordinators all chose to leave at the end of 1996, along with the only woman driver. They mostly attributed their decision to the high level of insecurity, coupled with the fact that they could not have their families with them.

left The only woman driver among 21 employed by Oxfam in Ikafe

Oxfam/Jenny Matthews

Among refugee staff, there were other influences preventing women from applying, among them an implicit understanding that, where jobs were available, they should be reserved for men; and there was pressure from men, who were sometimes jealous to guard their positions within the household. Faisa R. explained:

> ❩ It is seen as a man's right to work before a woman's, and so women should not be competing for jobs with them. In Sudan, it was only two generations back that all government jobs were reserved for men. So when jobs are few, a woman does not question the right of her husband or brothers to go up first. ❩

There was also the practical problem that women in Sudan are generally less well educated; although there were some well-qualified women around, they were thinly spread among the various agencies, and tended to prefer activities like health care and education.

In an effort to improve the gender balance, Oxfam went out of its way to recruit women. Yet for those who lacked the necessary technical, managerial, or social skills, the pressures of work limited the degree to which management could provide them with the support they needed to upgrade skills. It was rarely possible for newly recruited people to go off to attend relevant courses.

Better living conditions, possibly close by but not actually in the bush, would have given staff the chance to bring their families with them. Family-friendly policies which provide for home leave could have worked to attract more women staff. But most such personnel policies cost money, especially entitlement to leave from such remote areas; in Ikafe there simply was not scope in the budget to offer regular home leave, especially when expensive air travel was often the only safe way out of the District.

Local recruitment

Recruitment is always a highly political issue, especially where job opportunities are few and there is mistrust between tribes (or castes). Accusations of nepotism within Oxfam increased local tensions. The following excerpt from a letter from the LC4 Chairman in Aringa County to the Settlement Commandant in January 1996 illustrates the importance accorded to it by local leaders:

> ❧ The Aringa people comprehend the refugee resettlement programme in Aringa as investment whose other important effect is employment for both the Local and foreign population … Aringa county is capable to provide most of the required elite, drivers, cooks, watchmen, masons, carpenters etc. that you need. It surprises us to see that you have imported most of your employees to the extent of even getting drivers, turn-boys and others from somewhere … This deprivation of employment is one cause of isolation — that is why we think your programmes are foreign policy. ❧

It is true that Oxfam had 'imported' staff to fill positions at lower management levels which could perhaps have been filled locally; drivers are the prime example (although one quarter still came from Aringa County, and over one third from Arua District). But Oxfam's policy in Uganda has always been to create opportunities for existing employees wherever possible. Some drivers have been with the Uganda programme for over 10 years, moving with a particular vehicle from one emergency situation to another. They know Oxfam's ways of working and are also trusted. They also all have a good command of English to communicate on the radio, which is vital for insecure environments.

In fact, the movement of refugees into the District did create considerable opportunities for local employment. Of 195 contracted and temporary staff in 1996, 142 were from Arua District, 49 of these — around a quarter — from Aringa County, and 19 from Terego. The programme also provided considerable scope for casual labour — loading, cleaning, and construction work — in an area which had never had such opportunities. Of the casual labour force, 98 per cent were Ugandans from Aringa and Terego counties.

Perhaps, however, Oxfam had failed to pay sufficient attention to the conflicting interests of different tribes. Although almost three-quarters of staff were from within the District, it made little difference to the local Aringa. Many of those who later appeared on the 'hit lists' of local leaders were people from Arua District itself. As one Aringa explained:

> ❪ The ones making noise were local politicians, who wanted to become heroes of the people. The process of recruitment was very fair. Positions were well advertised and Aringa competed like any other ... Anyway, what would have happened if the programme had taken all Aringa? They would have drained the other areas, like schools, health centres, local government offices. Once the programme closed, then where would those people have been? ❫

In a politically tense situation, an agency needs to be completely confident that recruitment has been fair, and that systems are transparent. Where tribal mistrust runs high, it is also important to be sure that a programme or sector is not dominated by one group or another.

Employing refugees

Employment was a major concern for the refugees. Opportunities for earning a cash income in Ikafe were limited, yet many refugees had left jobs in Sudan with government, UNHCR, or other NGOs. Some were well qualified for the higher-grade posts, as agronomists, foresters, teachers, health staff, or community workers. They were keen to have more of a presence within the organisation to improve transparency, as there was much mistrust of agency management, especially of Ugandans from the District. The feelings of this Point Chairperson were typical:

> ❪ If we had a refugee employed as store man, then we would know that our food is not getting stolen. We would also get better received in the office. When we come to see an Oxfam person at the moment, we are made to wait and wait, and our problems are not taken seriously. A refugee would be working for his people, not just for the money. ❫

There are several good reasons, apart from improving transparency, for making sure that refugees are employed on programmes. First, it facilitates better integration between refugees and the programme staff. Second, just as employing more women at higher levels sends out a certain message, so giving refugees responsibilities within the organisation recognises their status as people, not as second-rate citizens. Apart from anything else, refugees have a right to work under the UN Convention on the Status of Refugees.[2]

Refugee managers: When Oxfam was obliged to evacuate its staff, the position was helped enormously by the existence of management structures which incorporated a good number of refugees at higher levels, many of whom had received extensive training over the previous two years. It meant there was a good skills base which remained with the refugee community throughout.

Yet it was not legally possible to employ refugees in Ikafe. The tax threshold in Uganda is very low: around US$130 per month. Any foreigner earning above this figure, and therefore paying tax, needs a valid work permit — which has been difficult for any foreigner to obtain, especially since the introduction of structural adjustment policies (SAPs), large-scale retrenchment, and the growth of the informal sector. Only a very few refugees have been awarded work permits. As a result, in Ikafe the Sudanese were only ever given minimal 'incentive' payments, which were not taxable.[3]

This not only undermined their professionalism, it also meant that Oxfam was effectively in a position to exploit highly trained workers. While refugee staff were in a position to collect food rations and use medical services provided for the refugee population, and though they were considerably better off than other Sudanese who were not employed, their benefits did not compare favourably with their Ugandan counterparts. Ugandan staff, though taxed, received substantially larger net salaries, as well as free food (for much of the time), medical benefits (for themselves and their dependants), and various end-of-contract benefits. In a culture like Uganda's, where money is so important, this did nothing to promote refugees within the organisation. Where they were not being paid the equivalent of local staff, it was sometimes difficult for them to earn equal status and respect from their Ugandan colleagues.

Extension staff: Oxfam had hoped from the outset to have extension staff who would be given training to upgrade their skills, and possibly bicycles to facilitate movement, but would otherwise be working for the community voluntarily. Paying them would immediately threaten to undermine future voluntarism at community level, and therefore the sustainability of activities.

Yet some sectors were having problems getting community work moving, and, once one sector had taken the decision to pay incentives, others had to follow suit. Referring to Community Health Workers, a member of staff commented:

> ❝ Once they became "Oxfam employees", they lost the incentive to do any voluntary work. It became like a proper job for them. They were "Oxfam employees", even though they were selected by the community, and the community had the right to de-select them. They came to be seen as the "working class", separated from everyone else. If there was voluntary work to be done, the community would turn round and say: "You're being paid, you do it yourself". ❞

The implications were all the more apparent as security deteriorated, and the extensionists were in a much better position to take care of themselves and their families. Sara K., interviewed when refugees were first displaced in Yumbe, explained some of the implications:

> ❝ First they came with new clothes and radios, which made some of us feel jealous. They put themselves above the rest of us. When [one extensionist] came back from a training in Arua, he even started walking differently ... Now here we all sleep under the mango trees, but they are not here suffering with us. They rent places to stay and are keeping dry; even their families are not with them here. How can they know our suffering? ❞

The appointment of paid 'community workers' meant that the very people who had formerly been leaders within the refugee communities — people who were chosen precisely because they were the most active and responsible within the community — had become separated and elevated above those whom they had at one time represented. Yet there had been a need for fast action. And getting community-based approaches going is difficult in any context, the more so in a situation like Ikafe, where community workers had grown accustomed to being paid in Koboko. The inherent contradiction came up again: capacity-building *per se* implied a certain approach that goes with operational work, and was not necessarily relevant to the style or pressures of relief work — which was the reality at that time.

It was expected that the prime responsibility of extension staff who were selected by the community would be to the community, rather than to Oxfam. However, in a bid to get the best people into the position, a number of extension staff — all agro-foresters and Community Facilitators — went through an interview process. The Community Facilitators in particular were often people who had previously been Point Leaders, but were then expected to stand down once they had been 'appointed' by Oxfam. It changed the dynamics of their role entirely. As a group of refugee staff have explained:

> ❝ An elected person in Sudan is never paid. In Sudan, it is all a local arrangement. People are chosen, such as the water point caretakers, and they are given training and tools necessary for their work. Like village midwives: they get nine months' training, and kits that are replaced. It could have worked here, if it had been done from the start. ❞

Because these were paid positions, professionals who were over-qualified were encouraged to apply, because there were very few other opportunities available. The refugee staff quoted above added:

> ❝ It is a matter of getting the right person for the right job. If you select a professional and ask them to do voluntary work, it is difficult. If, however, you select and then train, then they feel they have already gained something, and are more willing to continue it without payment. ❞

Exploiting volunteers?

As we have seen, the lack of opportunity to earn an income in Ikafe had a great impact on the perceived status and sense of self-respect of men in the refugee community. Oxfam was always keen to create opportunities for employment wherever possible, yet paying extensionists had far-reaching implications in other respects.

In particular, there was a danger that as payments were reduced, responsibilities would inevitably devolve on to a few individuals who were prepared to put in the extra time. In most communities, it is typically women who are cast as unpaid voluntary workers, and Ikafe was no exception. A Registration Clerk commented: *'We have often found it much easier to work with the women. Women are more prepared to do community work; some of the men have an attitude that they don't care. They always think of themselves first. We found women to be more dedicated and hard-working.'*

There was thus a danger that the limited 'free' time available to a few individuals might be abused, and that this might have an negative impact on their other responsibilities and on their domestic relations.

Alternatives to paid employment

A scheme was established in 1996 in which Point Leaders were given interest-free loans to acquire bicycles on credit. Bicycles are a valuable asset: they can be hired out, used to taxi materials and people, and in particular can provide access to markets in nearby towns to sell produce. They also confer a degree of status. As the Programme Co-ordinator responsible at that time commented:

> ❧ Leadership is enough. We should not have to pay community workers. People want respect. That is why it was so important for Oxfam to show them respect as well. Had we given bicycles to Point Leaders earlier on, it would have helped them in their work, and given them some status in the community. In that way, the two jobs of the Community Facilitator [a paid extensionist] and Point Leader could have been made one, because in many ways they paralleled each other. ❧

Some of the lessons learned in Ikafe about motivating refugee volunteers with incentives in kind are now being implemented in the programme in Imvepi. According to a Public Health Promoter: *'There are other ways of appreciating someone's work — food for work, or a bar of soap; something small, as recognition. They have always done it that way in Sudan for the TBAs [traditional birth attendants], for example.'*

Phasing out the employment of extension workers

Experience in Ikafe showed the importance of having clear understanding between the different Teams and between staff and refugees on the role of extension workers. Another Public Health Promoter explained:

> ❧ The policies on extension workers have to be overall and uniform, and they need to be made very clear; otherwise, when they are phased out, there will be demands. For health workers, we told them it was to be phased off, but other sectors took it as a job. One way would be to create a series of steps and gradually reduce the incentive. Then people might be more encouraged to keep going afterwards. ❧

Lessons learned in Ikafe are now being applied in Imvepi. Traditional birth attendants are working on a voluntary basis in Imvepi, although they had become accustomed to getting paid through AAIN in Koboko and Ikafe. Agricultural support services have been restructured, to replace a top–down approach with a more participatory scheme, in which most of the paid extension staff have been replaced by unpaid refugee Agro-Forestry Secretaries in every Point. A very few former refugee staff were retained for one year only, in order to co-ordinate activities. It was these Secretaries who did most of the seeds and tools distribution in July 1996, when Oxfam staff were evacuated. More recently in Imvepi, a few of the people who recently stood to be elected as unpaid Agro-Forestry Secretaries had formerly been Oxfam extension staff. It has proved that, in some areas at least, with good communication and a proper understanding between the agency and the community workers, it is possible to reduce staffing and still retain activities.

Policies to support staff (terms and conditions)

A complex programme like Ikafe poses particular challenges in terms of human resources. It was important that the systems which were set up to support staff did not work to undermine the direction of the programme. For example, because of the extremely remote location of the settlement, Oxfam initially needed to provide staff with meals, and other benefits more typical of relief situations. This led to high expectations among staff, and attitudes which were difficult to change, once funding was no longer available. This high-input, paternalistic style of management also sent out messages about Oxfam, to both refugees and staff, which did little to contribute to the programme's objectives of building up local capacity.

There was also the problem of where staff should actually live. A more stable town environment like Yumbe would have been more conducive to family life, which would have fostered independence from Oxfam. Yet the reality in Ikafe was that both government and UNHCR insisted on the office facilities being located within the settlement. In addition, experience in other refugee situations has shown that, if staff are located an hour's journey or more from refugee camps, they become segregated from the refugees. Oxfam always wanted to develop good relationships between staff and refugees, and to avoid establishing the traditional relationship of powerful donor and dependent recipient. Building up personal relationships was an important way of overcoming preconceptions on the parts of both refugees and staff.

Staff induction: Many of the staff who were employed on the programme by 1996 had been given no introduction to Oxfam's policies, nor to the goals, programmes, and strategies of Ikafe. Organisational priorities such as basic rights, gender analysis, participatory approaches, sustainable livelihoods, and the 'One Programme' approach were not properly understood, because people had been recruited in a hurry and started working in the field almost immediately. A training and induction had been carried out for a week with the initial staff when the programme began in 1994, but not all of these staff were retained. Those who came later received no such introduction.

As a result, only a few of the staff knew anything of Oxfam's approaches and ways of working, which did not help to develop the kind of staffing that was needed. A Distribution Monitor remembers:

❝ I joined the Oxfam family in 1994, but it was not until two years later that I understood what "working for a fairer world" really meant. Until then, I thought they were talking about a fairer world for the ones who are employed! ❞

Rest and recuperation: Ikafe was never designed as an 'emergency' programme, and putting staff on contracts suitable for 'emergency' workers would in many ways have contradicted its original objectives. Yet in reality, Ikafe came much closer to being an 'emergency' programme than an operational capacity-building programme. There was never any clarity on the status of staff, who were effectively working as emergency workers, with different needs from those of the established staff in Kampala, yet hired on the same contracts.

As a result, staff felt badly treated. They expected their contracts to reflect their family situations and the emergency nature of the programme: *'If you cannot have families with you, then it is not fair that we are given the same pay and leave entitlement as development workers in Kampala. Is Ikafe accompanied or unaccompanied? If it is too insecure to bring families in from far, how can they apply the policies of accompanied staff in Ikafe?'*, one staff member complained. There was no provision for rest and recuperation, and annual leave entitlement allowed no extra time for staff travelling home outside the District.

The fact that they could not see their families, or even contact them by telephone, was a major concern for staff, both men and women (who often had considerable domestic responsibilities). It was an added source of stress; as a member of the Ikafe staff recently put it:

❝ If we knew we could get to see our wives and children every two months, it would be all right. You could just keep going, waiting for that time. When it is like this, though, not seeing families for six or seven months, your mind and body begins to wander. ❞

It did not help to retain good staff, and there were very high turnover levels, especially at the upper management levels. Yet it would have been financially impossible to provide opportunities for rest and recuperation when airplanes were the only safe form of transport in and out of Arua District, especially for a programme with such high staff numbers. It was another question to which there were no easy answers.

Addressing hidden needs: A programme the size of Ikafe, with a contracted staff of 195 at its height, and similar numbers of casual labourers and refugees on incentive, needed to have someone dealing specifically with human resource issues. Instead, such matters were dealt with on an *ad hoc* basis, and certain particular needs, such as those of women staff, inevitably got sidelined. One female employee in Ikafe recalled:

> ❧ It was difficult to go to the Project Manager with some issues, but there were no women in top management. ... None of the women ever brought up their gender needs. We were all considered like men. Things like our monthly periods. No one thought about women's needs — but at times it was very difficult to travel to Arua in order to purchase items. ❧

Such cases are common where women are poorly represented. Changes necessary to accommodate gender-related needs in a working environment are more likely to happen if women are employed in senior management.

Accommodation for refugee staff: There were no positive policies or systems to ensure that refugee staff were treated equally and properly incorporated into the organisation, a fact which increased the divide between the refugee and national staff.

For instance, up until Oxfam evacuated in June 1996, refugee staff did not live in the Oxfam compounds. This had been a deliberate policy, to avoid increasing the divide between refugee staff and the community. However, this was perceived by refugee staff on higher grades as an indication that Oxfam did not value them as highly as it did the national staff: *'Already we were being paid less. Then they could not even provide us basic accommodation, even though we were told we were the same as regular staff.'* [4]

Now in Imvepi, refugee staff live together with Ugandan staff in the compound. This has had an important psychological impact: refugee staff feel more valued and see themselves as part of the organisation. It has also sent out a positive message to the refugee community: that Oxfam values the Sudanese as much as it values the Ugandans; and it has helped to bridge gaps between the two communities.

Personal development: For staff, the persistently uncertain future of the Ikafe programme made planning extremely difficult. Funding was guaranteed for short periods only, so staff were hired on renewable short-term contracts. The uncertainty made it very difficult to invest in things like training and staff development, and the job insecurity bought more stress to staff, which undermined motivation and work performance. As the Administrator in Ikafe put it: *'The paradox remains: how to motivate staff in a clearly uncertain situation such as this, when they are already aware of job losses and constantly fearing when rebels will next hit.'*

Staff stress

Staff were continually working under very stressful conditions in Ikafe, and the uncertain future and lack of clear personnel polices did nothing to reduce the toll on them. Initially working to very demanding deadlines to meet the refugees' basic needs, staff encountered aggression from people who felt that their needs were not being addressed. They also had to cope with the difficulties of working in such an isolated situation, and later on with the threat of a rebel attack or ambush on the road.

The following account by a Distribution Monitor illustrates the sorts of problem staff were having to deal with in the early days:

> ❩ You are forced to live separate from your family. You work all day in the field. In the early days you would start by 6.30–7.00 and not finish until after dark. Seven days a week. No time for recreation. It all accumulates in the end. Then the refugees we were working for were often quite hostile ... If food was delayed for more than a week, they would come with pangas, cut down trees, threaten us and so on ... So you get worried when WFP trucks have not arrived. You know you will have visitors. You have to go and explain to a hungry man. He can't help shouting at you. ❩

Later on, the problems were exacerbated by local politics. Another staff member recalled how the Local Council made a list of targeted staff, while others received verbal death threats:

> ❩ If your name is on the list, then you do not feel very happy. It does not make a good working environment. You are never sure what is going to happen to you. You do not know who is your enemy and your friend. This affects your work performance. ❩

As things gradually settled down, staff began to mix more with the refugee communities. Some attended religious services in the settlements, or they were invited to attend weddings, and a number began to make visits to refugee homes at weekends, as friends. This sort of relationship inevitably collapsed once security declined, particularly because security guidelines restricted staff travel. After Oxfam had withdrawn, things deteriorated further. The contrast between the position of staff who were able to get away from the risk of rebel attack and the situation of the refugees, who felt abandoned and extremely vulnerable, was very apparent. Oxfam felt it had no option but to put the safety of staff first, yet a number of staff felt an emotional commitment to stay close behind, to provide more care and reassurance. Many members of staff felt acute frustration and guilt felt at the time.

The insecurity increased tensions among staff, but again their needs were often marginalised. They were evacuated to Arua into very cramped conditions, where they slept four or five to a room, and tried to carry out work with no office facilities, mostly perched on beds or under trees within the compound, for almost a year. Yet for managers, it was almost impossible to take firm decisions on living conditions, because the future was so unclear.

Throughout the period of the insecurity, managers consistently had to take very difficult decisions on issues of staff safety, as they struggled to find a balance between addressing refugees' needs and ensuring staff safety. While identifying with the refugee community and having a sense of responsibility for their welfare, they also had to consider Oxfam's obligations and responsibilities for staff welfare. This invariably threw up extremely difficult questions. A senior manager mused about the use of male and female staff in difficult circumstances.

> There was a time when local young men were being abducted around Yumbe, while there had been no incident of women being targeted in the same way. Yet we took the decision to keep women from the field, because of the risks of rape. We were aware that, by having an all-male staff in the operational team following evacuation, we were putting the gender aspects of the programme at risk. How would we know how women refugees were really coping without having people in the field they felt they could approach? Also, were women staff simply dispensable like that? But in the end we felt the risks outweighed the benefits. If the rebels suddenly changed tactics, and a woman staff was raped, we would have too much to answer for.

As tensions built up, people tended to drink and party more than usual. Many established close personal relationships. Although condoms were available, very little attention was given to promoting good health practice, because staff welfare was not always prioritised. In such a closed environment, the risks of contracting diseases are increased. In 1996 and 1997, more than nine members of staff or former employees were lost to HIV/AIDS-related illnesses. Some of them had formed relationships with refugees, and some with other members of staff.

The shooting in Bidibidi was an extremely traumatic experience for most members of staff, and later on, as they moved between Yumbe and Arua, or when living in Ikafe, they often felt under threat. Yet their feelings were never openly discussed. Men and women have different needs, especially in times of insecurity, and different ways of coping. There may be fewer informal mechanisms for men to deal with trauma, as well as cultural expectations that they should be less affected. The effects of emotional trauma may be expressed in all sorts of less obvious ways. Yet there was very little attempt to discuss the effects or monitor staff stress at all.

Some staff felt that more tangible things could have been done to support them. One person commented:

> ❦ Management need to give a rest to staff after they have been through an attack. It lowers morale. People will feel that you as a manager do not consider them. That you are only interested in output. You do not care about his personal feelings. ❧

This was accentuated by an apparent lack of concern for employees who had lost personal property after the evacuation:5

> ❦ After the looting, staff expected Oxfam to contribute. But there was a lack of clarity. Some people who had lost money in ambushes got compensation; but there was no budget for the cumulative property of all the staff in Bidibidi who were looted. We did not have any proper insurance. It really made staff lose heart. ❧

One thing that Oxfam did do was to emphasise training. Over 130 field staff and refugee extensionist staff were given training in communication skills, and some carried out PRA work in less affected parts of the District. This was valued by staff at the time, and helped to raise morale. For refugees, it was also a chance to get a rest from never-ending insecurity, but there were added strains of being separated from their families at times when attacks were still imminent, which had to be considered.

In conclusion:
some lessons and recommendations

8

Would Oxfam have embarked on the Ikafe programme if all the ensuing problems could have been foreseen? The short answer must be yes, despite the great strain which it placed on the agency's resources, and despite the fact that, on the face of it, there is very little to show for the enormous investment of time, people, and funds: hardly any of the settlement still stands today. Yet, in the words of a member of staff at the head office: *'In our heart of hearts, we wanted people to go back home. It should not be seen as a failure when people return.'*

There is no doubt that the settlement gave more than 50,000 people the chance of a more dignified life while they chose to stay in exile. For many, it offered a vision of a better future. Many of the refugees now in Imvepi look back on their time in Ikafe before the rebel attacks as 'the golden years'.

Oxfam's vision for Ikafe was to make the dignity of the refugees central to the whole programme; and to take into account the rights and interests of the local population. These values have not been called into question. However, although self-reliance was seen as the key to the restoration of dignity, in the circumstances it was perhaps never a feasible objective. Similarly, the principles which guided implementation — participatory planning, good communication, gender-awareness, and concern for the environment — were ideals. Experience in Ikafe demonstrated the difficulty of making them a reality in a programme which always remained an 'emergency', and where staff had to engage in a constant struggle to work in sensitive and creative ways.

Ikafe was an innovative programme, and many of the lessons presented in this book have been applied, either during the lifetime of the Ikafe programme itself, or now in Imvepi: lessons about the need for representative structures, shared management of resources, and improved communications. Much of the lobbying to increase the size of land allocations, and the work to agree on more realistic objectives and appropriate programme inputs, served to consolidate the basis of Oxfam's operations in Imvepi. Some of the broader policy issues which were identified and documented, such as site suitability or the impacts of food insecurity, are relevant to many other situations.

Oxfam learned much, too, about organisational issues in turbulent contexts: the need to be realistic and to accept that situations are ever-changing; the need to develop contingency plans and provide safety nets; and the need for flexible support systems. Lessons were learned about the importance of understanding and accommodating indigenous systems, and creating opportunities for gender-related concerns to be heard. And there were broader lessons about ways of working, communications, and advocacy.

Institutional concerns

Looking back, one of Oxfam's Emergencies managers observed: *'Ikafe began as a refugee camp and not as a settlement. Because of the circumstances, it was essentially a humanitarian response to an emergency situation.'* It could be said in retrospect that Oxfam set off on the wrong foot in Ikafe. Nothing was in place before the refugees arrived, so it was impossible to plan with any degree of realism. The assessment of agricultural potential was going on at the same time that farming was being started; land and compensation issues were still being negotiated after the land had been occupied.

Yet the objectives remained unchanged. Ikafe was always presented to donors as a sustainable option — although it was never really clear that self-reliance was feasible. In the opinion of another Emergencies manager:

> ❧ In some ways we were victims of our own rhetoric. By saying we were going for sustainability and self-reliance, we gave the donors a let-out clause. It was much easier for them to turn round and withdraw funding when we appeared to be off-line. It also undermined the refugees' right to receive assistance, if it proved impossible to attain those objectives in the longer term. ❧

Short-term objectives

Without a realistic assessment of the situation in which they are operating, it is impossible for agencies to identify the right sort of programming. It may be that they should set themselves less ambitious objectives for relief work and operational 'development' programmes in turbulent contexts; perhaps they should seek instead to concentrate on ways of building up the capacity of the communities they are trying to support.

Building up assets: Recognising that refugees may want to return to their homeland in a relatively short space of time, programmes should perhaps concentrate more efforts on identifying what could be done to support them in the interim: building up assets, giving training, providing education, at the same time as meeting their basic needs. When Ikafe first began, it was assumed that the refugees would stay in Uganda for anything between one and five years; the future was always dependent on the fluctuating wars and insurgency on both sides of the border. But their sojourn would probably be long enough for at least two planting seasons, and there would be time enough to set up small businesses. More than anything, people needed short-term measures which would help them to meet their needs in a dignified fashion.

Respecting people's priorities: Thinking about issues from the refugees' perspectives is important. In Ikafe, education was always one of their main priorities; they were also interested in developing some sort of livelihood for themselves. Although for many this did not extend to long-term agricultural self-sufficiency, short-term crops and vegetables became particularly important as the situation deteriorated, as did access to credit. In a refugee context, the conditions for 'development' may never be met, but agencies can and should identify the conditions for building up the capacity of the community, and take advantage of them.

Reducing vulnerability: When the settlement became insecure, Oxfam learned the importance of having mechanisms to reduce the refugees' vulnerability to food shortages and violent attack. It was useful to have in place right from the start some short-term measures which would provide safety nets if and when conditions deteriorated: good systems of representation, for example, and community-based distribution schemes; systems for credit which allowed for small, high-turnaround, low-risk loans; and research going on within the community which enabled staff to understand the issues and respond in more relevant ways.

Bridging the gap between 'relief' and 'development'

For any agency, trying to build up capacity from a base of emergency relief work requires a considerable degree of pragmatism, a sense of realism, and the ability to remain flexible. In the current climate, it is increasingly unhelpful to pigeonhole programmes as either 'relief' or 'development'.

In situations of extreme instability, when funding is uncertain and there are threats to the physical security of the programme, nothing is ever really 'normal'. For emergency workers in south Sudan, for example, instability is the norm, yet the programme of response may be of a long-term nature. Perhaps the terms 'relief' and 'development' should be redefined to take account of the concept of 'working in turbulent contexts'.

Flexible systems

The need for reliable information. In the early days of Ikafe, when the emphasis was on fast action and high-input programming by a largely technical staff, time was often the scarcest resource. There was nothing like the space provided by a 'normal' development programme to enable a participatory approach to planning, implementation, or evaluation. In such contexts, a commitment to an on-going programme of action-research is vital. In Ikafe, a team of refugee extension staff was trained in techniques of action-research, and a professional sociologist was employed to co-ordinate their work in the field and communicate the findings to management. There is no point in doing action-research if the commissioning agency cannot recognise the need for change and act on the researchers' recommendations, once it has reached a better understanding of the cultural, political, and economic dynamics of the situation.

Whistle-blowing: In Ikafe there were no alarm bells built into the programme to alert managers when things were going off-track. Following the detailed assessment of the carrying capacity of the land, for example, the settlement should have adopted a less ambitious set of goals. Again, after displacement, there was a need for new objectives, ones which took into account the refugees' own fears and priorities, and their narrower horizons. The programme needed a consistent way of checking that it was still on the right track. One member of staff commented: '*I often think that operational programmes take on a kind of life of their own, and once they are up and running it can be very difficult to reorient them.*' Where objectives cannot be met, the fact should be made explicit and the programme adapted.

The participatory review: The process of the review in 1996 was particularly helpful, in that it gave a chance to people who had been closely involved in the programme for almost two years to reflect on their own priorities, and those of other players. In Ikafe, fundamental concepts like self-sufficiency and host–refugee integration had always been interpreted by different people in very different ways. The review gave an opportunity for people who hoped to benefit from the programme to meet directly with donors and government officials, and for each to get an idea of how the others would define success. It also helped Oxfam to define more realistic objectives for Ikafe, ones which took into account the priorities of the various stakeholders.

Phased activities: Agencies must be realistic about the funding base on which they are operating. In an ideal world, for example, funds would be committed for three to five years, but in reality donors operate on one-year plans. So agencies must think seriously about the level of commitment they are able to make. They may need to consider phasing their activities. In the words of an Emergencies Department manager: '*There is a danger of building a road that ends in the middle of a field. Programmes may need to think about making compromises initially, in order to do a programme that is more feasible.*'

Human resources

Besides a pragmatic approach, constant monitoring, and the ability to adapt to changing circumstances, working in turbulent contexts needs good, committed staff, with the right sorts of 'people skills', and the dedication and flexibility to work in difficult circumstances. Oxfam's Uganda Representative comments:

> ❛ If we were to do this again, I would pay much more attention to systems and staffing, and gear up to ensure that the systems were good ... [to] free up management to attend to the programme. I would pay closer attention to long-term funding and sources. I would emphasise development experience for senior staff over operational emergency experience. ❜

Attracting staff: An agency's ability to attract high-calibre staff (and keep them) can make or break a programme. Yet, as Ikafe showed, it is often hard to recruit people with the right sort of approach at short notice and in such a remote and unstable situation. Family-friendly policies, and opportunities for staff development, may help to attract and keep good staff. It was difficult in Ikafe to achieve a good gender balance, and especially to bring women into higher management posts. In such situations it might be necessary to consider positive discrimination in recruitment to improve the gender balance, but this policy must be accompanied by additional training, if applicants are lacking in any respects.

Support for staff: Field staff who have never been involved in anything but very direct emergency relief work may need help in understanding concepts like participation or gender; and training should be followed up with assessments of how staff are actually performing in the field. Separate personnel policies may be necessary, to meet the needs of staff in protracted emergencies. Refugee staff are likely to have particular needs.

Managers should be given training to identify and respond to signs of stress among staff. It is particularly important to adopt a conscious policy of promoting public-health messages to staff, and making condoms readily available.

Management structures: High-input relief activities tend to work best with a sector-specific approach, yet an integrated way of working is the key to a transition towards longer-term development. In Ikafe, things became much easier once management structures had been realigned into teams of field staff and extension workers, and the teams were given regular opportunities to share ideas and discuss workplans.

Local recruitment: Employment can become a political issue. If there had been more time for Oxfam to gain an understanding of the dynamics of the local population, the employment issue might have been handled more sensitively.

- Importing fewer staff for non-technical roles, such as drivers or distribution monitors, might have reduced tensions, though in reality the local Aringa politicians were demanding mostly higher-grade jobs.

- Recruiting refugees into higher management posts helped to build trust between refugees and Oxfam, and ensured that programme activities continued when most Oxfam staff were evacuated during the insecurity. In some cultures, refugees will rarely be accorded proper status, or treated as equals, unless they are paid the same as local staff.

- Paying incentives to Sudanese refugees in Ikafe served in many ways to undermine voluntary activities. There are other forms of incentive, such as training, which may encourage people to contribute their time to work for the community. However, agencies must beware of allowing the burden of voluntary work to fall disproportionately on to women.

Programming

Rebuilding communities

Registration: During a recent exercise, a group of refugee staff ranked problems of poor registration as the most fundamental obstacle to successful settlement in Ikafe. Good registration, which takes into account the different needs of refugees, especially the need to be settled close to relatives or members of the same ethnic group, or on land that can support their livelihoods, is valuable in ways which may not be immediately apparent. If pastoralists had been registered separately, for example, they might have been accommodated on land more suitable for cattle-grazing, which would have helped them to rebuild their livelihoods.

- Family tracing is a high priority for refugees, especially for psychological and social reasons. Keeping personal records on electronic databases can facilitate family reunions.

- Allowing movement within the settlement, accommodating the needs of polygamous households, and helping single women or other vulnerable groups to settle close to relatives or kinspeople can be vital in the process of reconstructing social systems. Communities in Ikafe might have benefited from less tight filling of the Blocks: initially perhaps four plots in every 24 should have been left free, to facilitate later transfers.

- Providing valuable non-food items on a *per capita* basis, rather than a household basis, would have discouraged people from registering separately and then later applying for family reunion.

Representation: Good representation depends on respect for the social and political organisation of the communities. Adopting a system which is apparently more democratic may undermine the very social relations and institutions which are vital for rebuilding capacity. In Ikafe, during the year of extreme insecurity, it was the indigenous tribal systems which proved to be the most durable.

However, while it is important to accommodate traditional systems, it is equally important that a system of representation creates opportunities for women to express themselves and assume roles of responsibility. 'Encouraging' equal representation is often not enough. Promoting women's involvement more actively by ensuring an equal number of positions for women and men in fact created a more representative and genuinely consultative structure, albeit one which was imposed by Oxfam.

It was useful in Ikafe to put temporary structures in place initially, which could be adapted and modified once a clearer picture of the social and political dynamics of the refugee population had been built up; and while the members of the community got to know each other. Establishing temporary structures initially can benefit women in particular, because they are often too busy in the early stages of resettlement to stand for elections, or even at times to attend meetings.

Gender matters: No agency should assume that gender-related concerns will be addressed simply because they are included in a programme's objectives. A carefully thought-out strategy, with clearly defined commitments and responsibilities, is essential to enable managers to monitor their work from a gender perspective.

Every activity contains gender-related aspects. Meeting apparently everyday needs often brings unexpected benefits. In Ikafe, women reported that the provision of cloth for menstruation, for example, increased their self-respect, and with that their readiness to participate in the programme.

Having a member of staff solely responsible for gender issues might have helped to keep them on the agenda, but the emphasis should always be on developing the skills of all staff, to enable them to analyse and incorporate gender-related concerns in all sectoral activities.

Vulnerability: In a context as unstable as Ikafe, the nature of 'vulnerability' changes frequently. It was useful to have a team trained in skills of participatory analysis, to help staff to understand who was at the greatest risk at any particular time, and why. For example, female-headed households may not necessarily or always be the worst-off: women and children in other family structures may be more vulnerable.

- The terminology used in the programme may influence people's attitudes. Labelling people as 'vulnerable' is likely to make them feel much less able to help themselves.

- When dealing with traumatised people, it is important not to undermine traditional healing processes, and to recognise that Western-style one-to-one counselling may not be the answer to their needs.

- It is important to carry out as early as possible a comprehensive interdisciplinary professional analysis of the needs of physically disadvantaged people (for spectacles and other appliances, for example). Helping disabled people to meet their physical needs can give them a big psychological boost not only to them, but to the whole community.

- It was useful in Ikafe to have one member of staff responsible during periods of displacement for locating the more disadvantaged people and documenting their needs. Such needs are otherwise liable to be overlooked in a crisis.

Flexibility: Longer-term objectives of capacity-building may need to be set aside temporarily during periods of insecurity, because the situation will demand short-term means of giving support, such as buying up seeds to prevent distress sales at very low market prices; or providing additional items for shelter, or tools and seeds for cultivation. It may be necessary to re-establish higher external inputs during times of insecurity and when refugees first arrive, because community networks will probably have collapsed, especially for people from minority tribes, women who have recently been raped and possibly deserted, and men who have been left alone with dependants and are thus unable to go in search of food or work.

Viable settlements

Environmental sustainability: High levels of cultivation will never be sustained, for either refugees or their hosts, if the population has expanded rapidly; yet for hungry people the harmful effects of intensive cultivation on the local environment tend to take second place to the immediate gains. There are ways to encourage refugees to take part in conservation activities, if the focus is on short-term gains, such as food or cash income. Livelihoods do not operate in an economic and social vacuum, and, in addition to a commitment to protect land for future use, there must be guarantees of access to land and the rights of local people to develop their own livelihoods.

- Access to land is central to ensuring sustainable livelihoods, and land rights should be clarified early on. Site surveys should identify potential problems of tenure, and negotiations should ensure that the local population are fully aware of what will be entailed if they donate their land. It is important to identify any sacred sites, and to clarify all boundaries before demarcation. Cultural practices, especially ceremonies connected with sacred sites, must be respected as far as possible by agencies and refugees.

- Thorough physical surveys should always be carried out on the ground before the programme begins. They should include tests of soil quality at a range of sites, details of current occupancy, and an inventory of all natural resources.

- Site surveys should also assess off-farm income opportunities and the scope for cattle-rearing, if the refugee population is from an urban or pastoral background.

- Surveys should also include a thorough socio-cultural and political assessment of the area and its inhabitants.

- Surveys should seek the views of everybody who is involved in or affected by the settlement programme. This is likely to include local people (elders and political or administrative representatives), refugee representatives, the government, UNHCR, and any implementing partners in a joint consultation exercise.

- It is important to be clear right from the start about who will benefit from wood-lots, especially when they are initiated and managed by an agency. Wood-lots should be handed over to the local community at the earliest opportunity. Individual distribution should be closely monitored and followed up with expert technical advice within the community.

- Taking precautionary measures is always better than having to start the process of re-planting. Demarcating greenbelts and marking certain trees of cultural or environmental significance is an important aspect of natural-resource management.

- It proved useful in Ikafe to have environmental monitoring teams consisting of both refugees and local people. If new influxes are expected, it is helpful to have a contingency plan, so that new arrivals are included in conservation schemes right from the start.

- Environmental concerns cannot be addressed in an institutional vacuum. Sound practice should be integrated into every aspect of programming. Agencies should beware the possibility of inadvertently giving the wrong messages, and strive to set good examples in such matters as the use of wood-burning stoves in agency kitchens, and sustainable methods of constructing housing for staff.

Rebuilding livelihoods

Food policies: The persistent shortages of food in Ikafe consistently undermined refugees' attempts to achieve self-reliance. The more they were obliged by delays in food delivery to organise distress sales, the weaker (and therefore less able to dig) they became, and the less able their children were to attend school, because they needed to look for work and wild food. When WFP responded to the delays by providing buffer stocks to ensure more timely delivery, this had a hugely positive impact on the psychological and physical well-being of the refugees.

Distribution: It is important to establish where the balance of power lies in any system, and to explore ways of ensuring that the less powerful are properly supported. Distribution of emergency supplies is much better kept in the hands of the community. In particular, women should be targeted and included right from the start, and their involvement in the system regularly monitored. It may be more relevant in some situations to give women overall responsibility, and in others to ensure their equal involvement. Each system should be designed to suit the particular circumstances.

There must be continuous monitoring, using quantitative and qualitative data, to reveal perceived and actual patterns of access to food. Good communication between monitors and refugees is essential. Information about food distribution must be made available to the whole community all of the time, so that beneficiaries know what their entitlements are, and when they can expect to receive them.

Sustaining food production: It is impossible to set objectives for agricultural self-sufficiency if the resources to support it are not available. The minimum acreage required *per capita* must be agreed by all parties well in advance.

It should be remembered that food security is often an issue for the host population as much as for the refugees. Expanding extension services to include local people can help to improve good relations, as well as strengthening the local economy.

Short-term measures can be very important. Even during the insecurity, refugees in Ikafe wanted to cultivate. Those who had access to food crops were much less vulnerable to food shortages than those who had not. Quick-growing crops, such as vegetables and cowpeas, were popular in the transits for displaced people.

Research is vital. Participatory assessments should be carried out to identify people's priorities, their knowledge base, and traditional practices. Refugees themselves should take part in crop assessments, so that they are part of the process of eventually transferring responsibility for livelihoods from agencies to the community.

Sustainable livelihoods: Self-reliance in the true sense of the word will always involve every aspect of refugees' lives and livelihoods. Settlement sites need to cater for off-farm activities, because people from urban and commercial backgrounds have needs quite different from those of refugees who want to cultivate. Good economic opportunities, especially infrastructure for marketing, are essential to both. Pastoralists have their own needs, especially for adequate grazing land and paraveterinary services.

Providing credit can reduce refugees' vulnerability to food shortages. It is important to identify changing opportunities and recognise that markets continue to function even within relatively disorientated communities.

Agencies may need to lobby to improve the legal status of refugees if they intend to promote viable economic activities. Will the laws of the host country undermine people's capabilities for becoming self-reliant? Are refugees free to trade? Are they exempt from paying taxes? Can they legally set up their own markets? Are they permitted to travel outside the settlement?

Communications

The high-speed/high-input nature of many refugee programmes limits the opportunities for participation in planning; in reality, agencies are often obliged to adopt a reactive role and focus on meeting basic needs. One way to avoid conflict and misunderstanding is to reach agreement with all parties on the programme's objectives before it begins. If a firm commitment has been made to a jointly agreed set of goals, there is always a base-line position to refer to, if problems arise in the future.

- Once objectives have been agreed, time-frames and monitoring methods should be established.

- Implementing agencies should take advantage of their pivotal position to encourage dialogue at different levels and between various parties. Forums should be established for refugees and nationals to discuss issues such as shared resources, land allocation, and security.

- Good public relations at the local level are essential. If a programme does not involve the local community in planning, it risks being isolated from the physical, social, and economic realities on the ground. The host population should be engaged in regular dialogue, to demonstrate that the agency values their views. It is a good idea to appoint a representative to act as the link with the local community. In Ikafe, local people, employed by Oxfam to act as Community Officers, did useful liaison work.

- It is vital to ensure that refugees have access to information about matters such as food deliveries and security threats which will enable them to make strategic decisions. Ideally such messages should be directed to the whole community, but in reality they will probably be spread via community leaders — who may need transport or access to radio contact, if physical constraints make dialogue difficult.

Advocacy work

Advocacy work is vital, and should be integral to all programming. The welfare of refugees depends not only on operational projects, but on efforts to ensure a favourable policy environment.

Advocacy on behalf of the refugees in Ikafe was done at a number of levels: international, national, and local. It was sometimes formal, presenting documented evidence of the impact of certain policies; and sometimes informal: a casual request for additional resources. It may be appropriate to do some lobbying on longer-term issues from the agency's head office, in collaboration with other agencies if they have problems in common.

- If an agency is to lobby effectively, it must have access to reliable information. Staff may need training in the collection and analysis of data for advocacy work.

- Transparency is vital. It is much easier for any agency to lobby if it has always been open and willing to share information with other stakeholders.

- It is important to ensure that all staff are aware of their agency's policies on particular issues. Often it is those who work in the field in stressful conditions who may be tempted to compromise in order to keep operations going. If they understand the commitments and policies of other agencies involved, and the core values of their own agency, staff are more likely to have the confidence to do lobbying work.

Donor support

The extremely insecure nature of funds for Ikafe limited Oxfam's ability to plan for the long term, and necessitated constant revisions in the budget. This meant that programming was often guided from the top down. It damaged staff morale and reduced their commitment to exploring more radical ways of working.

Funding for local infrastructure was limited, but expectations were extremely high, which led at times to political conflict. In such contexts, donors should seriously consider making a firm commitment to supporting local development, to ensure the social and economic viability of the settlement.

Measuring impact: Donors must be realistic, and adopt policies which make allowances for the turbulent context in which programmes like Ikafe are operating. Negotiations between donors and implementing agencies should recognise, in the setting of targets, that not everyone will achieve self-sufficiency in agriculture at the same time, and provision should be made accordingly.

Flexible funding: Programmes like Ikafe are unpredictable, because they do not operate in a political vacuum. Donors should be prepared to take risks, to fund the uncertain, to remain flexible, and allow for change when the situation demands it. This may mean reverting to the provision of humanitarian relief if conditions deteriorate, whether because of insecurity, or poor harvests, or something else unforeseen.

Staying prepared: The ultimate aim is to rebuild communities from the bottom up, but realism is always the watchword: in many parts of the world, tribal, political, economic, or environmental factors make conflict or disaster inevitable. In some areas, especially in the turbulent regions of the Great Lakes and East Africa, agencies need to be prepared for trouble to strike at any time. Oxfam was able to respond to the initial calls for assistance in Ikafe only because it had infrastructure — human, material, and financial resources — already in place in Uganda.

'The rhetoric was right ...'

This book does not question the basic concepts and values which guided the Ikafe programme. Its practices and ways of working were important in and of themselves. But the programme illustrated what can happen to those ideals when they are exposed to the forces of hard reality.

Projects of such complexity need above all to be approached with realism: there is no substitute for proper scenario planning, good monitoring systems, and a readiness to adapt and at times to make compromises. Ikafe showed that, given a chance and the right kind of support, refugees are willing to make a fresh start and assume responsibility for their own futures. If the circumstances had been more favourable, it is quite possible that the programme would have made a significant difference to the refugees' attempts to rebuild their lives with dignity.

'... but we needed to be more realistic'

As it was, every time refugees were reaching a stage where they could begin to meet their own needs and think about the needs of others, the settlement was thrown into turmoil. Yet such turbulence is a reality in many parts of this region — and not just in refugee contexts. In Uganda, for example, structural adjustment policies and the HIV/AIDS epidemic have brought huge social changes. This fact calls into question the conventional definitions of 'relief' and 'development' work. Factors such as climate change, deteriorating terms of trade, and the breakdown of extended-family support mechanisms all work to create an extremely unstable environment, where outcomes cannot be determined, even in regions apparently free from overt forms of conflict.

The challenge to humanitarian agencies is to develop flexible responses to changing conditions. In the words of Oxfam's Country Representative in Uganda at the height of the Ikafe crisis: *'Normal is not normal. There may be "models", but they are only attempts to conceptualise an ideal picture of what reality is. Reality is ever changing and always different.'*

Notes

Chapter 1

1 This organisation changed its name in 1996 to Action Africa Hilfe (AAH). It is referred to as AAIN throughout this text.

Chapter 2

1 For more insight into the breakdown of traditional values and practices in Sudan, see Levine 1997.

2 In fact, there are international commitments to provision for host populations. The EC included provisions under Lomé III and IV for funding integrated programmes to minimise disruption to the local populace and to guard against disparities between the local population and refugees, especially in terms of health, education, and community facilities.

3 There is a strong political movement within Aringa to break away from Arua and create a separate District of 'Upper West Nile'; it is believed that the provision of such infrastructure could help to influence the decision.

Chapter 3

1 It had initially been hoped that AAIN would use the Public Health Secretaries within the 'Oxfam' structures. However, these were not approved by AAIN, because they were voluntary, and therefore perceived as untrained and lacking the necessary technical expertise.

2 The system was introduced into Ikafe from other programmes in East Africa where Oxfam has been distributing relief food. Donor agencies, especially WFP, have always questioned the method, and debate about its merits continues at a number of different levels.

3 More detail is given in an unpublished paper by Lina Payne (1997): 'Improving on Community-based Systems of Food Distribution', Kampala: Oxfam GB.

4 For more details of UNHCR policies on the protection of vulnerable women, see Anderson 1994; and UNHCR (undated).

5 It is always important, when adopting such terminology, to consider how it corresponds with use in local languages.

Chapter 4

1 A 'sustainable livelihoods' approach would normally encompass all the resources at the disposal of a household, and would include programming to develop human resources, namely health and education, which are hardly touched on in this text for reasons of lack of space. Oxfam only recently took on responsibility for education in Imvepi, and the health programme was just beginning to operate when insecurity struck. It is still too early to draw many conclusions.

2 However, full demarcation of forest reserves in Ikafe was achieved only on paper, as pressure to settle more people meant that settlement areas tended to encroach on boundaries.

3 The new draft land law has a specific section concerning the legal status of gazetted land.

4 For a more detailed picture, see articles by Lina Payne in *Field Exchange* and *Gender and Development,* listed under 'Sources and further reading'.

Chapter 5

1 Admittedly this is extremely difficult, because, although UNHCR is committed to the principle of long-term support, in reality, like the majority of donors, it cannot guarantee stipulated levels of funding for long periods.

2 For more information on the impact of food insecurity, see the article by Lina Payne in *Field Exchange,* listed in 'Sources and further reading'.

3 It is worth noting that, at the time of writing, and for the last six months of 1997, WFP provided buffer stocks within Ikafe settlement, which meant that food shortages were no longer an issue.

4 In an internal document published by WFP: 'Food Aid in Emergencies', first edition, Rome, September 1996, pp A6–6.

5 Personal conversation.

6 The UN Convention on the Status of Refugees: Articles 17–19 require that refugees are accorded the most favourable treatment for wage-earning employment, self-employment, and the practice of liberal professions.

Chapter 6

1 In addition, UNHCR's stated primary objective in refugee situations is voluntary repatriation.

2 For more information, see Neefjes and David: Review Report 1996. An article by Cromwell, in *Journal of Refugee Studies* 1:3/4 (1988), discusses the question of conflicting goals.

Chapter 7

1 A full account of the participatory review, written by Ros David and Koos Neefjes, is available with Oxfam. It contains more detail of some possible indicators and suggests ways of collecting them.

2 As noted in Chapter 5, Articles 17, 18, and 19 respectively provide for the most favourable treatment of refugees in wage-earning employment, self-employment, and the practice of liberal professions. Yet under the Control of Alien Refugees Act of 1960 which currently guides refugee policy in Uganda, there are restrictions on refugees taking up employment, although with certain permits they are allowed to travel outside gazetted areas and, in certain circumstances, to initiate businesses.

3 UNHCR funded minimal incentives, which Oxfam topped up to the tax threshold.

4 As noted above, the reason for the lower rates of pay offered to refugee staff was that MoLG would not give work permits to refugees for employment in posts not on incentive.

5 Oxfam does have policies to ensure that staff are compensated for loss. In this instance, the costs of compensating over 120 people were obviously considerable. As a result, the issue is still under discussion, and every effort is being made to ensure that staff do receive some compensation for property lost.

Sources and further reading

Adoko, J and L. Payne (1997) 'Gender and representation in Ikafe', *Links* (June 1997), Oxford: Oxfam GB

Anderson, M.B. (1994) 'People-Oriented Planning at Work — Using POP to Improve UNHCR Programming', A UNHCR Handbook, Geneva: UNHCR

Ayoo, S.J. (1997) 'From Relief to Development: Consequences of Local Settlement of Refugees on Host-Refugee Integration and Refugee Impoverishment. A Case Study of Ikafe Sudanese Refugees in North-Western Uganda', MA dissertation, School of Development Studies, University of East Anglia

Harrell-Bond, B (1986) *Imposing Aid*, Oxford: Oxford University Press

Harrell-Bond, B (1994) 'The Ikafe Refugee Settlement Project in Aringa County — A Report to Oxfam', unpublished report, Oxford: Oxfam GB

Levine, I. (1997) 'Promoting Humanitarian Principles: The Southern Sudanese Experience', *Relief and Rehabilitation Network* Paper 2

Needham, R. (1995) 'Refugee participation', *The Courier* No.150

Neefjes, K. and R. David (1996) 'A Participatory Review of the Ikafe Refugee Programme — Review Report', unpublished report, Oxford: Oxfam GB

Payne, L. (1997) 'Improving on Community-based Systems of Food Distribution', unpublished report, Kampala: Oxfam GB

Payne, L. (1997) 'The impact of food shortages on refugees in Ikafe/Imvepi', *Field Exchange*, Dublin: Emergency Nutrition Network

Payne, L. (1998) 'Coping mechanisms and vulnerability in situations of food insecurity', *Gender and Development* 6/1

Thirkell, A. (1995) 'The Community Development Programme in Ikafe Sudanese Refugee Settlement, Aringa County, North Uganda', unpublished report, Kampala: Oxfam GB

UNHCR (undated) 'Policy on Refugee Women, Report of the Executive Committee of the High Commissioner's Programme', Geneva: UNHCR

WFP (1991) 'Food Aid in Emergencies', WFP Handbook, first edition, Rome: WFP

White, P. (1997) 'Consultancy Report', unpublished report, Kampala: Oxfam GB

White, P. (1997) 'Working Against the Odds : Women Working in an Insecure Environment', MA dissertation, Human Resource Strategies, London Guildhall University

Yu, H-W. (1996) 'Final Report on Selected Bibliography of Refugee Settlements in Africa', prepared for Oxfam UK/I, Oxford: Refugee Studies Programme

Oxfam Development Casebooks

This series provides detailed case studies of individual Oxfam-supported projects and programmes. Each of these lively and accessible books draws on the views of Oxfam staff, counterpart organisations, and local communities to analyse successes and failures and to identify learning points for the future.

Other titles in the series include:

● **video for development**
  A Casebook from Vietnam
  Su Braden with Than Thi Thien Huong
  ISBN 0 85598 370 1

● **disabled children in a society at war**
  A Casebook from Bosnia
  Rachel Hastie
  ISBN 0 85598 373 6

● **empowering communities**
  A Casebook from West Sudan
  Peter Strachan and Chris Peters
  ISBN 0 85598 358 2

Oxfam GB publishes a wide range of books, manuals, and resource materials for specialist, academic, and general readers.

For a free catalogue, please write to:
Oxfam Publishing
274 Banbury Road
Oxford OX2 7DZ, UK
telephone 01865 313922
e-mail publish@oxfam.org.uk

We welcome readers' comments on any aspects of Oxfam publications.

Please write to the editorial team at:
Oxfam Publications
274 Banbury Road
Oxford OX2 7DZ, UK